SAM CHAMBERLAIN'S MEXICAN WAR:
THE SAN JACINTO MUSEUM OF HISTORY PAINTINGS

SAM CHAMBERLAIN'S MEXICAN WAR:

The San Jacinto Museum of History Paintings

By William H. Goetzmann

Published for the San Jacinto Museum of History

BY THE TEXAS STATE HISTORICAL ASSOCIATION, AUSTIN

Library of Congress Cataloging-in-Publication Data

Goetzmann, William H.
Sam Chamberlain's Mexican War: The San Jacinto Museum of History Paintings / by William H. Goetzmann

p.   cm.
Includes bibliographical references and index.
ISBN 0-87611-131-2 (cloth).—ISBN 0-87611-133-9 (limited).

1. Mexican War, 1846–1848—Art and the war—Catalogs.   2. Chamberlain, Samuel E. (Samuel Emery), 1829–1908—Art—Catalogs.   3. Watercolor painting, American—Catalogs.   4. Painting, Modern—19th century—United States—Catalogs.   5. San Jacinto Museum of History—Catalogs.   I. San Jacinto Museum of History.   II. Title.

E415.2.A78G64 1993
973.62—dc20
93-21480
CIP

10   9   8   7   6   5   4   3   2   1   93   94   95   96   97   98   99

Published for the San Jacinto Museum of History by the Texas State Historical Association in cooperation with the Center for Studies in Texas History at the University of Texas at Austin. Funded by a generous grant from the Summerlee Foundation, Dallas. All illustrations in this book are courtesy of the San Jacinto Museum of History unless otherwise noted.

The paper used in this book meets the minimum requirements of the American National Standard for Permanence of Paper for Printed Library Materials, Z39.48—1984.

Cover: *Company E, Dragoons, Fighting, Buena Vista* (detail) by Sam Chamberlain. Watercolor on paper. *Courtesy San Jacinto Museum of History.*

Frontispiece: *Sam Chamberlain Dreaming* by Sam Chamberlain. *Courtesy West Point Museum.*

Dedicated to Rusty Kelley and his dad, Brooks R. Kelley

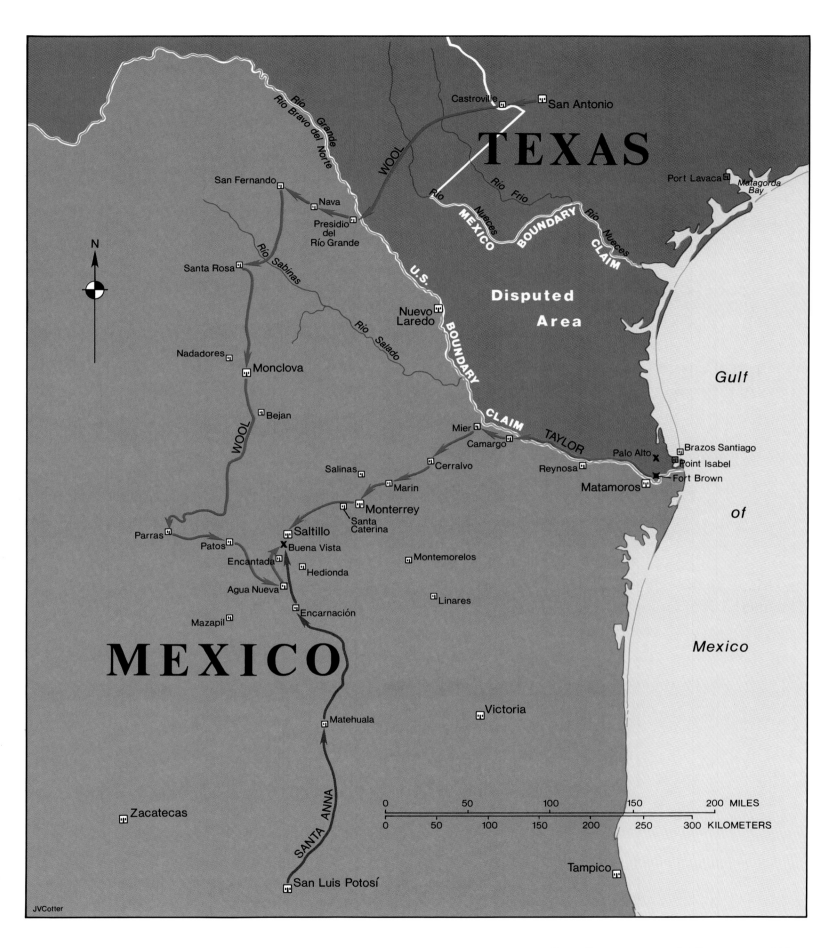

SAM CHAMBERLAIN'S THEATER OF WAR

CONTENTS

Acknowledgments IX

Foreword XI

Introduction 1

Notes 31

Suggestions for Further Reading 37

The Paintings 39

◆ The Battle of Monterrey 51

◆ The Battle of Buena Vista 111

Index 199

ACKNOWLEDGMENTS

THIS BOOK is due primarily to the enthusiasm of three men: Judge David Jackson of the Summerlee Foundation, which generously supported the project; J. C. Martin, director of the San Jacinto Museum of History; and Ron C. Tyler, director of the Texas State Historical Association. Judge Jackson is certainly the most enthusiastic student, not only of the war, but also of Sam Chamberlain. J. C. Martin and his assistant, T. J. Zalar, spared no effort in providing the basic materials for this book, especially the pictures that form the heart of the work. Dr. Ron C. Tyler, a good friend, has shepherded this project along, as well as provided advice and inspiration. These three leading patrons, together with scholars John Crain, Ben Huseman, and David Weber, even traveled to Mexico for an on-site inspection of Monterrey, Saltillo, and Buena Vista, photographing the battle sites—which the present author appreciates, having made the trip himself much too long ago.

I also wish to thank Michael Moss, director of the West Point Museum, and David Meschutt, curator of manuscripts there. Peter Harrington, curator of the Anne S. K. Brown Military History Collection at Brown University, has been of great help in locating a number of hitherto unknown Chamberlain paintings of the war in the Brown Collection, some of which are included in this book. For permission to use them, we give grateful acknowledgment. Tom Kailborn, another expert on the Mexican War, has been helpful in sharing not only his materials but his considerable expertise. Mrs. George Dameral of Portland, Maine, Sam Chamberlain's great-granddaughter, has also been of immense help, not only in explaining family traditions and discerning the fate of others of his descendants, but also in coming up with eight beautiful Chamberlain watercolors and some draft pages of his manuscript book, *My Confession*.

Dr. Nancy Anderson, assistant curator of American art at the National Gallery of Art, was also helpful. Col. Merle Moore did yeoman service in digging out records from the National Archives that I could not get to on my own trip there.

I am also indebted to Milan Hughston, librarian at the Amon Carter Museum, for his help and the Museum in general for lending a photocopy of West Point's *My Confession*. The latter, of course, is indispensable to this and a second Chamberlain project to follow.

I have greatly benefited from critical readings by Professor Harwood Hinton, John Eisenhower, and Professor Robert Johannsen, as well as telephone conversations with Professor Ralph Smith of Abilene Christian College and Cormac McCarthy of El Paso, Texas. And I must not forget John Crain of the Summerlee Foundation, who has done so much to facilitate this project. His research and his encouragement have helped me much more than one could find in the footnotes.

My personal research staff, in part paid for by my Jack S. Blanton, Sr., Chair, at various times has included Ben Huseman, who not only transcribed the manuscript *My Confession* but also wrote detailed commentaries on the materials used and the condition of the San Jacinto paintings. He also found the title page to the San Jacinto album, thereby dating it far differently than did the dealers at the Old Print Shop, who sold the album to the San Jacinto Museum in 1956. Huseman has also been of help in correctly identifying scenes in some of the mislabeled San Jacinto pictures.

Others who aided me greatly as part of my research staff were David Baird, who researched Chamberlain's Arizona and Baja California adventures at the Arizona Historical Society Library and Sam's prison records as warden of the Connecticut State Prison at Wethersfield. In the latter, he had the help of the Connecticut State Library at Hartford. David also found a clue which was the key to my interpretation of Chamberlain's work on his manuscripts in discovering the work of William Ainsworth, one of Sam's favorite writers. William Pugsley conducted "the dredging operation" of locating all collections that might have Chamberlains and contacting their curators. In addition, he has located some interesting commentary on how Sam ran his prisons at Charlestown, Massachusetts, and Wethersfield, Connecticut. Sandra Selvia went through microfilm reels of the *Daily Alta California* chronicling William Walker's trial. My administrative assistant, Mary Harmon, coordinated much of this activity and made numerous phone calls to libraries and typed the correspondence, as well as the drafts and final copies of my manuscript, which has proven to be a fascinating but grueling exercise in detective work. George Ward and Martin Kohout labored over the formidable task of editing, and John V. Cotter created the maps.

I also wish to thank especially my wife Mewes, who managed to put up with me and a littered family room while I worked.

FOREWORD

ON OCCASION I have been urged to put the whole saga of the search for Sam Chamberlain and the provenance of his various albums in my introduction. It is indeed a remarkable story and yet an unfinished one, as my footnotes indicate. Upon careful reflection, however, I have decided that this book belongs to Sam rather than to me. Thus many of my reflections concerning the questions mentioned above are in the extensive footnotes. I have been told that "nobody will see them buried in the footnotes." That may be true. I hope it isn't. For a model, I look back with great respect to Robert Taft's *Artists and Illustrators of the Old West,* wherein the notes "buried" at the end of the book make the most exciting scholarly reading imaginable. They have provided leads to legions of scholars and collectors. Since mine is a more specific project, I cannot pretend that my footnotes will match the impact of Taft's. I do, however, urge readers not to skip them. They do have a story of their own to tell and, equally important, they raise the many questions that I have been unable to answer in my quest for Sam Chamberlain's various texts or albums. I, of course, hope that they will inspire anyone with further knowledge of General Chamberlain's literary and artistic materials to come forward with whatever information they care to share. Already some twenty-two exquisite renditions of another version of *My Confession* have come to light, suggesting that there is a whole set of Chamberlain watercolors still to be located. In this volume, I have included many of these for comparison with those in the San Jacinto collection.

Maps of the Battles of Monterrey and Buena Vista are placed with Chamberlain's paintings of those crucial events in the Mexican War. Locations of other places mentioned by Chamberlain can be found on the general map on page vi.

I would point out that Sam's story is not finished with this book. The next phase of our Summerlee Foundation and Texas State Historical Association project is the reprinting of Chamberlain's *My Confession* from the illuminated manuscript at West Point exactly as he originally wrote it. This has never been done. Sam's chronology, even his veracity, is questionable on many points, and the previous editor of *My Confession,* Roger Butterfield, tinkered with the original manuscript in a valiant attempt to separate truth from imagination. Thus, much of the original does not appear in the 1956 Harper's and *Life* magazine versions. Moreover, Butterfield felt it necessary to correct Sam's atrocious spelling and to switch around sentences so as to make for popular reading.

Our task in reprinting the original volume is, alas, further complicated by the fact that since the publication of the Harper's edition of 1956 numerous pages, including Sam's description of the Battle of Buena Vista, in which he actually participated, are now missing from the manuscript. We wish whoever has them would come forward with them. Sam deserves better treatment, given his lifelong labors on his beautiful works.

And finally, several people have suggested that I provide a complete history of the Mexican War in my introduction instead of merely sketching out the campaigns, as I have done. Such an undertaking is far beyond the scope of this book, though I do know a great deal about the war and its aftermath, as readers of my previous books will know. To present a whole history of the campaigns clearly would bury Sam when, in fact, despite his bigotry against Mexican males (never females!), I came to praise him. Sam, not the war with Mexico, is the star, the artist/writer/creator. Even now other scholars, particularly Mexican scholars with new access to the Mexican National Archives, are rewriting the story of the war. While I look forward to their published work, I have to say that my subject is Gen. Samuel Chamberlain, an enigmatic, creative, and almost forgotten imagineer.

WILLIAM H. GOETZMANN
The University of Texas at Austin

SAM CHAMBERLAIN'S MEXICAN WAR

S AMUEL E. CHAMBERLAIN has lived too long in obscurity. At six feet two inches tall and sporting the long golden locks of a cavalier, Sam was only fifteen when he went off to a war that became almost as obscure as he has been since his death in 1908. This would be the War with Mexico that took place from 1846 to 1848. In the 1940s, nearly one hundred years later, Sam began to emerge—back from the dead, so to speak. It seems that he had written and illustrated an unpublished military masterpiece, *My Confession,* aptly subtitled "The Recollections of a Rogue." This lost masterpiece, currently in the collection of the West Point Museum, finally saw the full light of historical day in 1956 when *Life* magazine published three installments illustrated by some of Sam's remarkable pictures, beginning on July 23, 1956. It was almost as if someone had discovered a lost first draft of *Huckleberry Finn,* illustrated in most animated fashion by Mr. Mark Twain himself.

Suddenly millions of readers of *Life* knew of Sam Chamberlain and his rollicking adventures in Old Mexico. Later in 1956, when a book-length version of his Munchausenesque adventures came out, published by Harper's and edited by Roger Butterfield, an editor of *Life,* still more of Sam's tale unfolded.[1] At the time most reviewers were enthusiastic in their praise of the book. Only Professor Walter P. Webb of the University of Texas, in a review published in *The Saturday Review,* called it a hoax, and Mr. Butterfield threatened him with a lawsuit.[2]

At the same time, an album of 147 watercolors also surfaced in the Old Print Shop in New York.[3] These, too, were unmistakably Chamberlain's roguish work. This album was soon acquired by the San Jacinto Museum of History, housed in the San Jacinto Monument, an immense structure on the site of the Battle of San Jacinto, where Sam Houston and a ragtag army defeated Mexican Dictator-General Antonio López de Santa Anna's startled army of professional soldiers and gained independence for Texas. The San Jacinto Monument, with its tall pylon and a Texas star on top, is taller than the Washington Monument in the United States Capital. This is very much in the spirit of that arch-romantic Chamberlain. He must even now, from his unmarked grave at Mt. Auburn Cemetery in Old Cambridge, Massachusetts, be pleased that his pictures and his adventures are on view so near the place where he turned from a boy "barely sixteen years old" to a man. In Texas he became a United States dragoon, and in the notorious Bexar Exchange in San Antonio he met up with the wild Texas Rangers and saw his first man die violently by bowie knife at the hands of the notorious outlaw John Glanton.[4]

This magnificently illustrated book, with its 156 Chamberlain watercolors and gouaches, is about these paintings, but it inevitably is also about Private Sam Chamberlain in America's forgotten war, with all the bloodshed and

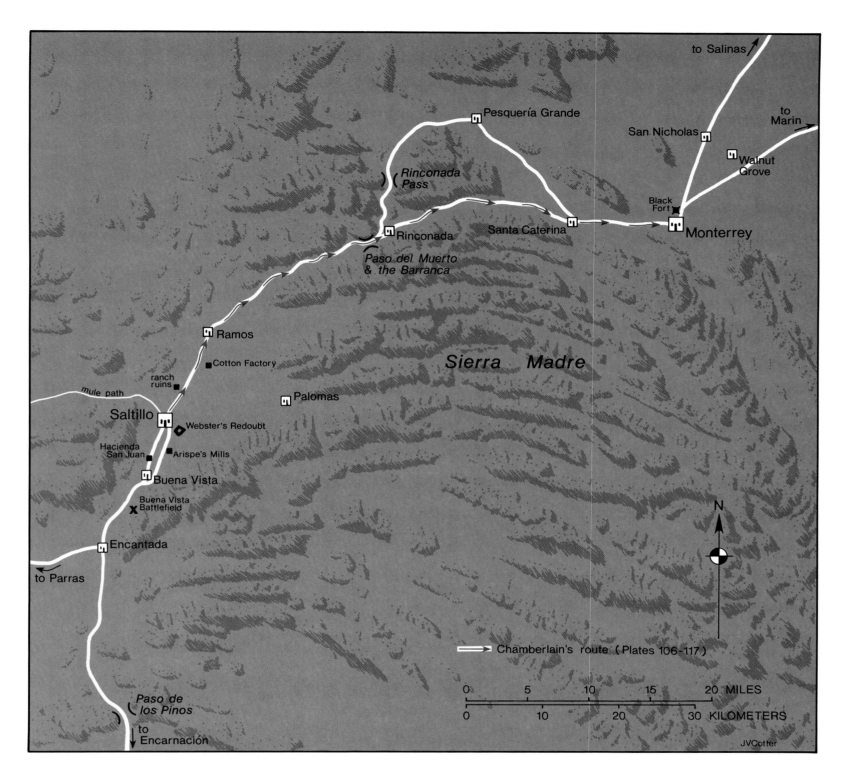

to Salinas

to Marin

Pesquería Grande

San Nicholas

Walnut Grove

Rinconada Pass

Rinconada

Black Fort

Santa Caterina

Monterrey

Paso del Muerto & the Barranca

Ramos

Sierra Madre

Cotton Factory

ranch ruins

mule path

Palomas

Saltillo

Webster's Redoubt

Hacienda San Juan

Arispe's Mills

Buena Vista

x Buena Vista Battlefield

N

Encantada

to Parras

⟶ Chamberlain's route (Plates 106–117)

0   5   10   15   20 MILES

0   10   20   30 KILOMETERS

Paso de los Pinos

to Encarnación

JVCotter

The Battles of Monterrey and Buena Vista

(see pages 51–65 and 111–141)

candid scenes of romance with enticing señoritas. It is also about the mystery of Sam himself and the circumstances of his work. This is not just another art book with amusing and sometimes gruesome pictures. Sam was not the American Goya. Rather, in the words of Chamberlain's contemporary, Walt Whitman, "Camerado, who so touches this book touches a man!"[5]

I.

The Mexican War, 1846–1848

OFTEN OBSCURED by an avalanche of enthusiasm for the American Civil War, the conflict with Mexico nevertheless was of the greatest importance to both countries. The United States gained and Mexico lost California, Utah, Nevada, Colorado, Arizona, New Mexico, and, finally, Texas, which the U.S. had annexed in 1845. With all this territory, the United States nearly doubled its size in one stroke. Mexico not only lost all of this territory, but suffered the destruction of towns, ranchos, and the major city of Monterrey. It also lost well over twenty thousand men and was left in disarray and national humiliation. For Mexicans, the war will be forever termed "the war of the American intervention," its heroes the young cadets of Chapultepec who allegedly threw themselves over its high walls rather than surrender to American forces.

The United States, on the other hand, reached its highest point in the "glories" of "Manifest Destiny." The nation achieved not only a spectacular military victory but a North American empire, reaching from the Atlantic to the Pacific and dominating the Gulf of Mexico, if not the Caribbean. The war was a geopolitical triumph that included the securing of territories like Texas and California, which had been coveted by Britain, then the most powerful nation on earth. It also opened a broad "window" on the vast Pacific and the Far Eastern trade, which at the time was virtually Britain's private monopoly. Internally the most immediate gain from the war was the securing of immense mineral deposits in California, Nevada, Arizona, and Colorado. On December 5, 1848, less than a year after the signing of the Treaty of Guadalupe Hidalgo on February 2, 1848, and its ratification by Congress on March 10, 1848, came the startling news of the discovery of gold in California.[6] Thus began the Gold Rush, a migration of hundreds of thousands of gold seekers not only from the United States but from all over the globe, from German duchies and Siberian Russia to Australia. Even if Mexico had won the war with the United States, could it have resisted the tide of gold-seekers and maintained control of its far northern provinces? It always had at best a precarious hold on these neglected and dangerous provinces filled with hostile Indians.

For Americans and Mexicans alike, the war at first seemed like a romantic adventure. Mexico had large numbers of troops, including gallant regiments of lancers resplendent in uniforms of "blue faced with red with waving plumes

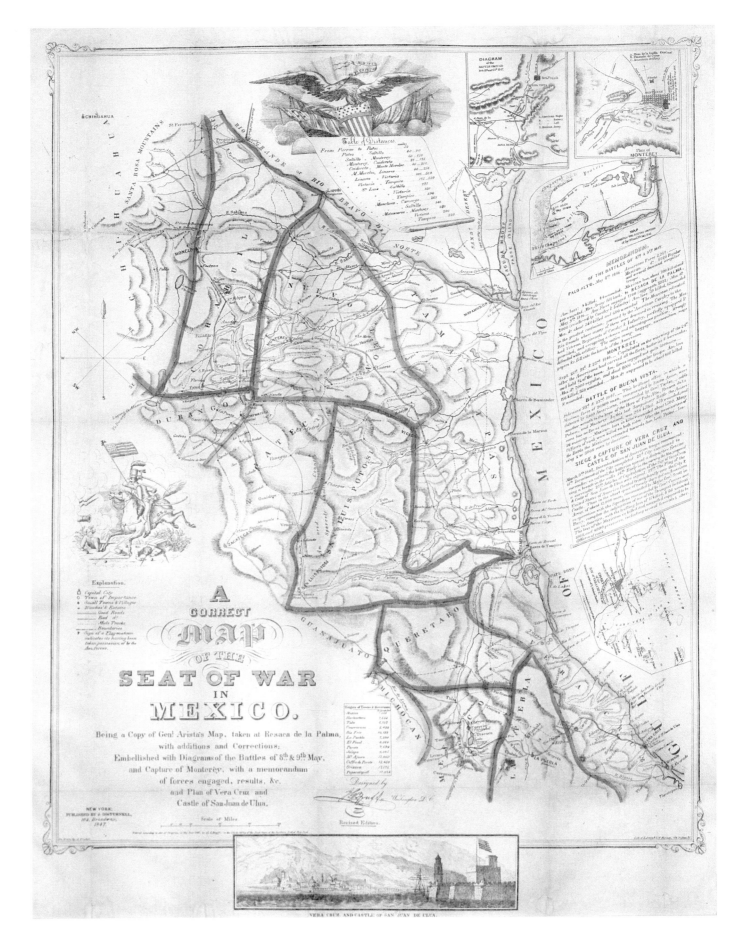

1-1. Mitchell's Map of the Seat of War in Mexico, adapted from map by General Pedro Ampudia

and glittering weapons" imported from Europe.[7] Its officers were caparisoned in the dazzling shades of Napoleon, to whom Santa Anna compared himself, and sat astride some of the finest prancing steeds ever bred. According to Sam Chamberlain, their uniforms were "white as snow, brasses and arms burnished until they glittered like gold and silver."[8] For once, Mexico's soldiers matched the sartorial grandeur of its clergy. To Mexicans and politicians like President Paredes, this new patriotic war was a chance to distinguish themselves, while at the same time teaching the crude and brutal gringos a lesson in the latest military tactics. Most Americans, too, overlooking the sad failure of their generals in the Seminole War in Florida, looked upon the coming clashes with romantic anticipation. Sam Chamberlain, our artist, was among them. It would never have occurred to him to agree with another Sam—the realistic Lt. Sam Grant, who, raised in an anti-war family, saw Taylor's army on the Rio Grande as a provocation and in his *Memoirs* remembered that he "was bitterly opposed to the measure," though in his letters while with Taylor's army, he seems intent only on doing his duty and returning to his fiancée as soon as possible. Grant, though he never brought up politics in his letters on the eve of war, apparently saw the United States as the stronger and Mexico as the weaker nation and the whole war as unjust.[9]

It is hardly clear that the United States was the stronger nation, though even then it possessed far greater industrial potential; nor is it entirely clear that it possessed a major military advantage, though its carbines were far superior to the Mexican escopetas, and recent developments in mobile artillery batteries and the training of artillery commanders made for a smaller but more powerful force on the open plain. Starting with a nucleus of fewer than 10,000 regular troops who could not even defeat the Seminoles, supplemented by 50,000 very green, sometimes obstreperous, three-month volunteers, and led by feuding generals who had never commanded more than a regiment, it was by no means certain that the United States would emerge victorious. The apparent bravado of the volunteers was in contrast to the attitude of generals Taylor and Scott, as well as Col. Alexander Doniphan and Brig. Gen. Stephen Watts Kearny, who had to lead these unruly green troops across thousands of miles of rugged desert and mountainous terrain into the heart of either Indian country or Mexico itself while depending on long, precarious supply lines vulnerable to Apaches, Comanches, and fierce Mexican guerrillas.

General Kearny, for example, led his men down the Santa Fe trail through Kiowa and Comanche country and conquered Santa Fe and Taos. Then he led a small company of one hundred dragoons through Apache country from New Mexico across Arizona to California, where he suffered a setback and wounds in the groin and buttocks in the Battle of San Pascual, after which, holed up at a place improbably called Snooks Ranch, he had to be saved by Kit Carson with one hundred sailors and eighty marines coming east across the Mojave Desert from San Diego.

This picture seems to include a guerrilla leader, a lancer out of uniform. Note the large Spanish spurs.

Colonel Doniphan early on cut loose from his supply line and led one thousand volunteer troops (later known in a classical reference to Xenophon's Thousand as "Doniphan's Thousand") directly south from Santa Fe. They struggled across the deadly Jornada del Muerto desert and, after battles at Bracito (El Paso) and Sacramento (outside Chihuahua), finally captured Chihuahua itself. But he had no backup or supply line. The latter was to have been furnished by General Wool marching west from San Antonio. Instead, Wool turned south and joined forces with Taylor's army in time to win the critical battle of Buena Vista.

General Taylor marched across the dry plateaus of northern Mexico and through mountain passes with a small army—mostly temporary volunteers—to incredible, and certainly lucky, victories at Monterrey and Buena Vista, where his force numbered 4,759 men versus Santa Anna's 20,000.[10] Taylor's army included the force led by General Wool, who had to pass through Comanche country as he headed across Texas from San Antonio.

Far to the south, coming out of the Gulf, Gen. Winfield Scott conducted a complex amphibious attack on what was regarded as Mexico's strongest position, Vera Cruz, with its massive fort, the Castle of Ulloa, where seven years before Santa Anna had repulsed a French invasion and lost his leg. Scott then had to take his men inland through mountain passes and the bloody Battle of Cerro Gordo to a series of even bloodier battles around Mexico City. In addition, none of the U.S. generals counted on the fierce guerrilla warfare waged by the Mexicans—a guerilla campaign about which Sam Chamberlain wrote almost constantly in his manuscript and portrayed in many of the pictures in this book. American occupation newspapers like *The American Star* and war correspondents, the first ever, wrote home lurid accounts of the guerrillas' hideous atrocities to newspapers like the New Orleans *Delta*, the Boston *Globe*, and Washington's *National Intelligencer*. Sam himself wrote:

> Woe to the unfortunate soldier who straggled behind. He was lassoed, stripped naked, and dragged through clumps of cactus until his body was full of needle-like thorns; then his privates cut off and crammed into his mouth, he was left to die in the solitude of the chapperal or to be eaten alive by vultures and coyotes. Such were the daily acts of the Guerillars [*sic*].[11]

The maverick diplomat Nicholas P. Trist, who had been dismissed by President Polk and routinely wrote seventy-five-manuscript-page letters to Congress,[12] secured the peace treaty at Guadalupe Hidalgo on February 2, 1848. Had he not done so, the American army of occupation may well have been ultimately defeated by disease, constant guerrilla attacks, a hostile civilian population, and political fire from the Whigs and Abolitionists back home.[13] Though "Old Rough and Ready" Taylor was deemed the hero of the war and elected

Clap Baylee   Mustang Grey   Jack Hays   Old Reid

1-3. Cap. Baylee, Mustang Grey, Hays, Old Reid
Watercolor, 6⅝ x 12⁷⁄₁₆ inches

Sam is here referring to Dr. Henry W. Baylor of La Grange, Texas, who served as a surgeon in John Coffee Hays's regiment of Texas Rangers in the Mexican War, then after Monterrey headed his own company of Rangers from Fayette County. Later he was stationed at General Taylor's headquarters.

Mustang Grey [*sic*] is really Mabry B. Gray, who was of the original Austin Colony. He participated in the Battle of San Jacinto and raised a group of raiders called "the cowboys." In the Mexican War he commanded a company called the "Mustangers." Gray gained his name when, while stranded on the prairie afoot, he killed a wounded buffalo, made a buffalo hide lasso or riata, and roped a mustang stallion near a waterhole. When he returned to camp, his companions dubbed him "Mustang Gray."

John Coffee, or "Jack," Hays, was a surveyor and a "noted Indian fighter," captain of a Texas Ranger company. He fought the Comanches from the top of Enchanted Rock, near Fredericksburg, and at Bandera Pass, Salado, and Plum Creek. In the Mexican War, he was a colonel in command of the First Regiment, Texas Mounted Volunteers, and distinguished himself at the Battle of Monterrey and the assault on Mexico City.

Old Reid is Ranger Samuel C. Reid, Jr., who in 1860 published his memoirs, The *Scouting Expeditions of McCulloch's Texas Rangers, or, the Summer and Fall Campaigns of the Army of the United States in Mexico—1846.* Reid's book may have served Sam as a source for his own account of the Rangers' activities at the Battle of

▶

1-4. TEXAS INDIANS
Watercolor, 3⅞ x 6¾ inches

These are Comanche chiefs under Santana, who rode right up to General Wool, reared their horses back, and lowered their lances while Santana, according to Chamberlain "a wolfish greasy cuss," rode up to Wool and, saying "how de do brudder," proceeded to crush Wool's small hand in his. Colonel Harney returned the favor.

◄

Monterrey. Later he attributes "fearful atrocities" to these men and to Ben McCulloch and Harry Love as well. They were accompanied by an old mountain man named "Greasy Rube," who had been castrated by the Mexicans in Chihuahua. At one point, "Greasy Rube" tied thirty-six Mexicans, one after another, to a pole and shot them, calmly cutting a notch in his rifle stock after each murder. This was way behind the lines at Camargo.

president by the Whig party, the real hero was the State Department's eccentric Trist—unless, by his own account, it was Private Samuel E. Chamberlain.

Sam was very definitely a roué, often a rogue, much of a boaster, and yet withal a soldier. He wrote, "When I first enlisted I resolved to discharge all duty prompt and faithful, and when off Duty [sic], I considered I had a right to enjoy myself as I deemed proper."[14]

Indeed he did, habitually filling his canteen with mescal and having affairs with señoritas almost too numerous to count. In cantinas, in open fields, and in houses of prostitution, he was, by his account, a regular swashbuckler at the code duello and romancing the señoritas. His *My Confession*, an illuminated, carefully handwritten book of 380 pages, now in the museum at West Point, amply chronicles both sides of Chamberlain's character at the time of his service in the Mexican War. Historian John Eisenhower, who has most recently studied Chamberlain, shrewdly observes that Sam "saw himself as a kind of Robin Hood, who though often caught in the wrong places, still always managed to prevail on the side of chivalry."[15] Eisenhower adds, "Captivated by the heroes of Walter Scott, he constantly throughout the narration, used all his 'strength and skill in defense of oppressed beauty.'"[16]

II.

Sam Chamberlain to the Life

THE PAINTINGS from the San Jacinto Museum collection reproduced in this book are in large part derived from notebook sketches by Chamberlain. Sam made them as he rode through Mexico with the First Dragoons, part of Brig. Gen. John E. Wool's army operation out of San Antonio. But what was his background and how did he find himself in Mexico? He was born on November 28, 1829, in Centre Harbor, New Hampshire, where his father was a stonecutter. When Sam was seven (1836), the family moved to Boston and settled near Bowdoin Square, where his father went into another business.[17] Sam attended the old Mayhew School on Chardon Street and sang in the Bowdoin Square Baptist Church choir. By the time he had reached fifteen, Chamberlain recollected in old age that thanks to Sheridan's Gymnasium he had become a "muscular Christian," who still wore long yellow curls while defending the ladies and beating the tar out of the Bowdoin Square Church choir director for insulting his girlfriend.[18] He then turned to the demimonde crowd at the National Theatre, where he hung out with "pugs," thespians, and Fanny the featured danseuse. All this time, and perhaps for the rest of his life, Sam pictured himself as one of Walter Scott's chivalric heroes, Ivanhoe or the Black Knight, though sometimes he remembered himself as Don Quixote.[19] He was always a "literary soldier." In actuality, when his father died in 1844, he became a Huck Finn and "lit out" West for Illinois to live with an uncle and his family at Skerritt's Prairie, not far from Alton, Illinois. There, after seducing several seminary school girls, pummelling his cousin, and giving his uncle a serious beating, nearly killing him with an axe, Sam "lit out" again.[20] He became a true rogue, in his own forlorn estimation; he had not gone far when he sat down on a log and "cried like a child."[21] Like Twain's celebrated character, he steamboated down the Mississippi, finding work at the state penitentiary at Baton Rouge.

So far his life, as recollected by the mature Civil War veteran Brevet Brigadier General Samuel Emery Chamberlain, read like the dime novels so popular at the time. Things got worse, however. He seduced convent-bred Stella Laboyce on the Baton Rouge levee. Her husband, an "old dried-up man of sixty" with "apelike features," got up a posse to hang poor chivalrous Sam. But once again, and just in time, Sam escaped his fate by hopping at the last minute aboard the *White Cloud,* "one of the great brag-boats of the Mississippi," which took him to safety at St. Louis.[22] An actor in a stage melodrama at Boston's National Theater could have handled it no better, but perhaps we shall never know whether Sam ever did it at all. One gets the impression that in older age Samuel Chamberlain, like Mark Twain, had some "things which he stretched," though perhaps like Twain "he told the truth mainly."[23]

We do know, however, from his military records that he lied about his age and joined the Alton, Illinois, Guards on June 12, 1846, one month after the outbreak of hostilities with Mexico, and, after leading a brief mutiny, set off with the Second Illinois Volunteer Regiment under Col. William H. Bissell for San Antonio.[24] We also know that, fed up with being a foot soldier or "doughboy," as such troops began to be called in the Mexican War,[25] Sam signed up with the First Dragoons in San Antonio. He stood before Capt. Enoch S. Steen of the First Dragoons and one Thomas Whitehead, chief justice of Bexar County, on the eighth day of September 1846 and lied his head off while under oath, claiming to be twenty-one years old—still with the sixteen-year-old cavalier's long golden locks.[26]

Sam found adventure aplenty fraternizing with the wild Texas Rangers in San Antonio. After observing John Glanton dispatch a Ranger with a bowie knife at the notorious Bexar Exchange, he acquired one himself—nine inches long, to be exact.[27] In no time at all he plunged it into his gambling partner and was tossed into San Antonio's old Spanish jail, which was infested with vermin and "blasphemous wretches who continually committed bestial orgies too revolting for belief."[28] Fortunately his "Arkansas toothpick" did not do in his erstwhile partner, who refused to press charges, and Sam was released. He fled, he says, chased by demons, and swooned "entirely nude" at Doctor Ritter's farm in Castroville, thirty miles west of San Antonio.[29] Naturally, he became "engaged" to the doctor's sister Katherine before returning to his regiment near Mission Concepción, where he was set to work cleaning up two feet of bat excrement that had accumulated on the ruined church floor.[30]

And so it went with Sam, according to Sam. It does not seem plausible, however, as Sam asserted, that he left San Antonio in late August accompanying Lt. James H. Carleton with dispatches from General Wool to General Taylor, which would have actually placed him in the Battle of Monterrey.[31] In reality, Carleton and Chamberlain marched out with the main body of Harney's Dragoons on September 25, 1846, passing through Comanche country to the Rio Grande opposite the Mexican town of Presidio, as was stated in the 1956 published version of *My Confession*. We do know, however, that he painted the Comanche warriors; vividly described their chief, Santana, as a "greasy cuss"; and also portrayed Harney's First Dragoons crossing the Rio Grande.

Following a skirmish with a crowd of fierce "guerillars," as Sam called them, and a pause at Agua Nueva, Carleton's command reached General Taylor's main camp at Walnut Springs, outside of Monterrey. In his manuscript recollections Chamberlain claims to have taken part in the Battle of Monterrey. Indeed, his account represents some of his best writing about a battle. But, alas, he probably was not there, though he painted plenty of pictures implying that he was in the thick of the battle along with the Texas Rangers who swarmed into the strategic Bishop's Palace.

After numerous marches and countermarches to Saltillo, Agua Nueva, and Parras, which included several narrow scrapes with guerrillas and the capture of a Mexican supply train, Sam reached the battlefield of Buena Vista, where he actually took part in the battle as part of General Taylor's escort and Col. Charley May's Second Dragoons, which included elements of the First Dragoons. His account of this critical battle is extremely vivid as well. Curiously, however, during the battle he seemed able to make sketches from all parts of the field, including one of Old Zach saying "a little more grape Cap. Bragg" (which he did not say) on the right flank and another pair of close-up scenes of the capture of O'Brien's battery (only three guns) and the stand of the red-shirted Mississippi Rifles on the left flank. Chamberlain also made several outstanding panorama sketches of the whole battle. From sketches like these he rendered, we don't know exactly when, the more or less finished watercolors in this collection. Nonetheless one has to agree with Eisenhower's assessment that "*My Confession* [and these San Jacinto paintings as well] stand alone and apart as the most vivid recording of what a soldier would see and feel as he trudged [or, in this case, rode his horse Soldan] down from San Antonio, Texas, to Buena Vista, Mexico."[32]

All of Chamberlain's wild chivalric stories and surreal pictures somehow represent the most convincing, if not amusing, account of the war. Such candid views as that of "Old Zach" jumping over a log for amusement and exercise must have come from an eyewitness situation. But he openly says that he got from hearsay the account of how Buena Vista was "actually" won—through the services of a "Yankee mill girl" who deliberately dallied with Mexican General Miñon at Saltillo and prevented him from cutting off all of Taylor's supplies. Could this be true? Well, yes, perhaps it could. We know that Santa Anna

'My maiden Charge' and how much I saw of the Thrilling affair.

I-5. SAM CHAMBERLAIN'S MAIDEN CHARGE
Pencil, watercolor and wash, 5⁵⁄₁₆ x 7¼ inches

Our hero is the one with the long curls in the center of the picture. Courtesy Anne S. K. Brown Military Collection, Brown University.

the next day disciplined Miñon severely for his "dalliances." Moreover, the New Orleans *Daily Delta* on June 16, 1847, revealed that "The gallant Mexican fell in with a lovely damsel at a factory near Saltillo, who so fascinated him, that, like Anthony in the arms of Cleopatra, he forgot all his military duties, and gave himself entirely up to the soft dalliance of love." The newspaper went on to add, "We give this story as told by the Mexicans about Saltillo, without assuming any responsibility therefore." On July 19, 1847, the same paper announced, "The following information, is based on an interview by the *Delta* with Dr. _____ Johnston, late of General Wool's staff. General Miñon had been released from durance vile into which he was thrown by Santa Anna, on account of that confounded love scrape at Saltillo." The reporter added, referring to Miñon, "He had a glorious opportunity at Saltillo and suffered himself to be enticed into an activity by a Mexican [*sic*] Delilah. . . ."[33]

It is these many close-up vignettes and even the hearsay and fantasy anecdotes that made Sam's story just plausible enough for extremely thorough but modern historians like Justin Smith, who wrote while Mexican War veterans were still alive, to use him as a historical source. Smith interviewed Sam himself—"the most sternly soldierlike" person he interviewed. Other historians of the war have used Sam's *My Confession* to good effect.[34]

After the fighting at Buena Vista was over, Sam spent some months at Walnut Springs, where he continued to fight guerillas and outlaws furiously, made himself at home in a house of prostitution in nearby San Nicholas, and rescued the beautiful Carmeleita Veigho [*sic*] from her brutal husband El Tuerto, whom he had previously humiliated. He, for the most part, enjoyed those months living with Carmeleita until they were interrupted by El Tuerto's kidnapping and murder of Carmeleita. One picture in this collection shows Sam riding through the night in search of his beloved. It is a dark and gloomy scene, suggesting that he had given up hope.

By July 18, 1848, he had been mustered out of the dragoons and joined, as a wagon master, Maj. Lawrence P. Graham's detachment headed for Tucson and California. This expedition included Lt. Cave J. Couts, whose excellent account of it has been published.[35] Major Graham, continually drunk, brutalized Sam. Lieutenant Couts's account of Graham squares with Chamberlain's. When they reached Tucson, however, Sam deserted and claims to have joined John Glanton's evil band of Apache scalp hunters, who had been commissioned by the Mexican government. After many dubious adventures with Glanton, including a trip to the Grand Canyon, which he was the first to paint, Sam headed for California.[36] He claims to have seen from a distance Glanton brained by the Yuma Indians, whom he had abused. Glanton had cut loose the Yumas' crude wagon-box ferry, killed O'Callaghan, the ferry master, and with his gang of desperadoes taken over Dr. Able Lincoln's ferry and made an illicit fortune.[37] Three of Glanton's men escaped: William Carr, Joseph Anderson and Marcus "Long" Webster. Sam claimed to have been with them—or he could, as an army deserter, have been one of them under an assumed name. At any rate, they reached San Diego after a difficult trek across the Mojave Desert. Sam, if he was telling the truth, went on to Los Angeles and then San Francisco. In 1853, after a hitch in the gold diggings, he was recruited by the notorious filibuster William Walker and took part in the attempted takeover of Sonora and Baja California.[38] Along with Walker, Sam was one of the relatively few who survived this ill-conceived operation. At this point, while Walker was tried and acquitted after a ten-day trial in San Francisco,[39] Sam Chamberlain disappears, though in a later piece of writing he regrets his foolish foray into Mexico with Walker.[40] Presumably he acquired considerable money, whether from gold from the California mines or from Glanton's San Diego bank deposit of money he made running the Yuma ferry. There was still another source Sam might have tapped. Rumors still abound that somewhere near the ferry site is a buried jar full of most of Glanton's loot—the lost Glanton treasure which Sam may well have found.[41]

Soon after the Walker debacle, Sam set off from Los Angeles, California, on a cruise around the world, during which he spent much time in the East Indies, the Himalayas, and parts of Africa. On this trip he made an extensive collection of exotic weapons that became the nucleus of an even larger collection, including Medieval armor, Indian bows and arrows, gleaming Napoleonic helmets, and all manner of antique weapons from Europe and early America, including a Puritan blunderbuss, which he proudly displayed in his "den" at his retirement home in Barre, Massachusetts.[42] Clearly, Sam had acquired a considerable fortune in California or Arizona.

After he landed in Boston in 1854, he married Canadian Mary Keith, whom, family tradition has it, he met on the boat coming from Scotland.[43] They settled in Cambridge and had three daughters, all of whom Sam named after the Mexican mistresses whose names he had misspelled: Carmeleita, Tranceita, and Delorious. For some years, according to Roger Butterfield and Henry Lee Higginson, he served as a teamster, fireman, and then a policeman in Cambridge. At the outbreak of the Civil War he joined the Third Massachusetts Militia, with which he served three months as a first lieutenant.[44] This was the first volunteer regiment raised by the Union. He then joined the elite First Massachusetts Cavalry, in which he was soon commissioned captain. The First Massachusetts was studded with famous Boston names: Charles Francis Adams II, some Bowditches, Crowinshields, and Higginsons, as well as Horace B. Sargent and his brother-in-law Louis Cabot, Lawrence Motley, and Charles A. Longfellow.[45] The soldierly Chamberlain rose through the ranks steadily from captain to colonel of the regiment and was breveted as a brigadier general for "gallant and meritorious conduct" in the Battle of St. Mary's Church on June 25, 1864. Sam's papers contain a handwritten map of the engagement.[46]

He claims to have taken part in thirty-five such engagements during the Civil War.[47] He claims he was near Manassas in August 1862 when he was surrounded by a cluster of Jeb Stuart's Confederate cavalry. He pretended to surrender, but instead plunged his trusty sabre clean through one of his captors and galloped through their encirclement to freedom. He was not so lucky at Poolesville, Virginia, where he was wounded and briefly captured fighting Stuart's cavalry.[48] While serving as chief of staff to Gen. W. W. Averell he was severely wounded at Kelly's Ford, Virginia, on March 17, 1863.[49] Sam, after a three-month stay in hospital in Massachusetts, appears to have taken part in the opening battle of the Gettysburg campaign at Aldie Courthouse, on June 17, 1863, and to have marched into Gettysburg with the Sixth Corps on June 31. He reached the battlefield on July 2 and served with Custer's cavalry on the right flank on July 3 during that bloody and decisive battle.

All that summer of 1863, his unit followed Lee south into Virginia and on September 12, 1863, he fought at the Battle of Culpepper Courthouse. Most of the summer Chamberlain and the First Massachusetts Cavalry participated in the Mine Run Campaign in Gen. J. Irvin Gregg's Fifth Corps. But in September Sam, now a major, was ordered to Camp Parole at Annapolis, Maryland. On March 5, 1864, he was promoted to lieutenant colonel in command of the First Massachusetts in the Union army reorganization of 1864, when all three-year volunteer enlistments expired. In short, Sam reenlisted at a higher rank and rejoined his regiment on May 26 as its commander.[50] In that spring and summer, Chamberlain led the First Massachusetts at the head of the Army of the Potomac into position around Cold Harbor. As the summer passed, he was heavily engaged in battle after battle. He was wounded at the St. Mary's Church engagement. But Sam continued to lead his men in such battles as Sheridan's Trevellion Station raid, Malvern Hill, Newmarket, Reams Station, Dinwiddie Court House, and Harkinsville on September 16. On September 30, 1864, he was ordered once again to Camp Parole at Annapolis. In December 1864, the First Massachusetts participated in its last engagement without Sam. His friend Maj. Horace B. Sargent was killed in that skirmish. When the regiment went into winter quarters at Westbrook House from December until March 1865, the regiment was reorganized into seven companies. When Sam returned in March, he returned as its commander—a brevet brigadier general.[51] He received his final discharge from the First Massachusetts on July 28, 1865. The war was over, but he accepted command of the Fifth Massachusetts Cavalry the very next day.[52] This regiment, composed of all black soldiers ("buffalo soldiers"), was sent to Clarksville near the mouth of the Rio Grande.[53] Its mission was not clear, because the surrender at Appomattox had already taken place, and, after that, the last battle of the war had been fought and won by the Confederates at Palmito Ranch on May 12–13, 1865. Led by the Confederate commander, Ranger John Salmon "Rip" Ford, the Texans forced the federals to flee seven miles afoot, outracing the mounted Confederate cavalry back to Fort Brown on the lower Rio Grande.[54] Perhaps Sam's Massachusetts troopers were sent to prevent prominent Confederates from fleeing to Mexico or to establish control of all Rio

Horrors of War

Out some miles from Saltillo on the Durango road, hid in a natural amphitheatre, completely hid from the great world without, lay the beautiful little town of Patos. The inhabitants were a quiet peaceful race, living by tillage and their flocks of sheep and goats. Our Squadron had often visited the place on corn details the forage taken being paid for by the Quartermaster. We were always received with kindness by the people whose simple manners, forcible reminded one of the primitive ages. We would bivouac in front of their church on the Plaza, while lovely little Poblanas in their picturesque costumes would crowd around making free gifts of fruit and Leche. At night they would be seen in all their glory in the Fandango room, and many a dark eyed Senorita of the place learned to love the Bold Dragoon her country's foe. On one occasion while the wagons was absent on a scout, a detachment of Texans Rangers under the command of Capt Bayley was sent instead. The Rangers with wagons reached Patos, pass through the place and halted half a mile beyond. One man stopped behind and entering a Pulqueria indulged in too much Mezcal, Insane with the firey liquor he entered the Church and tore down a large image of the Saviour, he fastened his Lariat around its neck, then mounting his horse, he galloped up and down the Plaza, dragging the Image after him. The people at first were so surprised at the sacrilege, that they offered no opposition to the act, but the sight of their beloved gray haired Priest, thrown down and trampled on aroused them to madness. The miserable wretch was lassoed, tied to a huge wooden Cross in front of the Church and flayed alive. His horse escaping found his way to Bayley's bivouac, who thinking something was wrong mounted up his men and dashed back to the place they entered the Plaza at speed, when they saw their miserable comrade fixed to a cross, his skin hanging in stripes, the place was crowded with the native inhabitants of the place gazing on the horrid sight. With yells of fury the Rangers charged on the crowd, with Revolver and Bowieknife slaying all they could, sparing neither age or sex in their fearfull revenge. The cause of all this was yet alive, and in his horrible suffering cursed all and everything and begged of his comrades to shoot him and end his torment. He was cut down and finding him beyond hope of recovery, a ball was sent through his brain by Bayley himself. The Church and buildings were fired, and Patos was among the things of the past. Capt Bayley made a report to Gen Wool, and the affair was hush up, no one was punished, for it was to disgracefull to the American arms, to be made known to the World.

I-6. HORRORS OF WAR
Pen and ink, watercolor, 13¼ x 7¾ inches

A chapter opening from Chamberlain's *My Confession*.

Storming the Bishops Palace.

1-7. STORMING THE BISHOP'S PALACE
Pencil, watercolor, gouache, 5 x 7¾ inches, careful writing verso

From the stories of the combatants who were actually there Sam has painted a masterfully dramatic view of the Texas Rangers fighting their way into the Bishop's Palace, a formidable Mexican stronghold overlooking the city. Courtesy Anne S. K. Brown Military Collection, Brown University.

Grande shipping, as well as frustrating raids by Canales's band of renegade bandits and a sizeable contingent of French troops. At any rate, the entire regiment was soon taken by ship all the way back to Boston and mustered out on November 28, 1865.[55]

Upon his return to Massachusetts, Chamberlain was appointed assistant quartermaster general of the State of Massachusetts in charge of the state arsenal on the staffs of governors Bullock and Claflin.[56] Then for ten years, from 1871 to 1881, he functioned as warden of the Massachusetts State Penitentiary at Charlestown and later Concord; then he served eight years, from 1885 to 1893, as warden of the Connecticut State Prison at Wethersfield.[57] At the Connecticut prison he became a controversial character, accused and later cleared of abusing prisoners.[58] One occasion of his service reveals warden Sam's way of dealing with unruly prisoners. Confronted by a knife-wielding convict who declared "he would cut the bowels out of the first man who laid hands on him," Sam coolly said, "Drop that knife." When the prisoner refused, Sam drew a revolver and said, "'I will wing you this time, but the next time you draw a knife on me you are a dead man.' Thereupon he fired, inflicting a flesh wound just above the elbow of the right arm. The knife dropped instantly from [convict] Burke's fingers and he was secured."[59] Though his philosophy was one of benevolence, there is some indication, beyond that of the Burke episode, that Warden Chamberlain was not beloved by all the prison inmates. One day he received an unsigned postcard from a former prisoner addressed to "Samuel E. Chamberlain, Brute Warden of State Prisons." The short message read:

> You miserable *Coward, Wretch*, brute! Devil incarnate! Though I do not believe there is a *Hell* worse than the one you preside over I could almost pray that there might be. So that such Cowardly Ruffians as you may at one time and for ever and ever get what they deserve. A thousand curses on your wicked head![60]

In 1893, after his exoneration, Sam retired to a rambling hilltop home in Barre, Massachusetts, where, surrounded by grandchildren, a huge collection of rare Bibles, his wife's fine china collection, and his own panoply of military weapons, he worked on the San Jacinto album of his Mexican War reminiscences. For some time Chamberlain attended virtually every Grand Army of the Republic and Massachusetts veterans function he possibly could.[61] He tried to become the very epitome of the Massachusetts soldier-hero and never missed an opportunity to make a speech. When he was not attending these functions, he filled his house with friends, taking them to his weapons-adorned den and regaling them with war stories and discussions of his various exotic weapons or stories of chivalry, which was his code to the end of his life. Near the end of his relatively long life, suffering did set in. The U.S. Pension Records of January 22, 1906, reveal that, according to Chamberlain, his right shoulder, broken by a "shell wound" in the Civil War, had become useless and he could not dress himself; nor could he do manual labor easily because of "a great weakness in his spine."[62] On November 10, 1908, he died of a heart attack in a Worcester hospital.[63] Some idea of his stature can be gained from his many published obituaries and the fact that he and his wife, who died in 1909, are both buried in Cambridge's Mount Auburn Cemetery, along with numerous other storytellers and immortals. A local poet wrote:

> He is not dead—this hero brave and true:
> He sweetly sleeps
> He's laid his armor off, his arms laid down
> And friendship weeps[64]

How much of *My Confession* is true and how much stemmed from Sam's amazing storytelling talents we shall probably never know fully, but even now a team of scholars at The University of Texas is hard at work trying to substantiate it and the incidents portrayed in the San Jacinto pictures, which follow in this volume. Surely Sam added to his exploits, but one clue as to his reputation for getting the story of the war straight is in a letter he received on March 25, 1903, from a New York novelist, Archibald Clavering Gunter, who in reply to Sam's criticism of his book wrote:

> Many thanks for what you say in regard to "The Spy Company." Of course, some of the incidents in it are, as you say, fiction, and in joining fiction with fact, it is impossible at times to have absolute historic accuracy with regard to all the real personages mentioned in a book . . . . However, I am glad the story interested one who was there at the time.[65]

This indicates that Sam was regarded as an authority on the Texas Rangers in the Mexican War, despite the fact that he was not with them at Monterrey. Given that he painted and wrote in the first person about his activities at Monterrey, a battle at which he was not present, Sam's implied reprimand of Gunter for inaccuracies is pure irony.

III.
The Album and the Paintings

THE PAINTINGS that make up the majority of the San Jacinto collection were in a large scrapbook resembling an old-fashioned ledger book covered in red-and-white upholstery cloth. There is also a haunting photograph of Sam on the title page as a very old, aristocratic-looking man seated in a rocking chair on his porch at his home, Maple Hall. In this, as in other pictures, he has a three-quarter pose with the badly disfigured left side of his face to the camera. This featured his most serious Civil War wound, one in which a minnieball had creased his nose, shattered his cheek, and lodged in his left scapula bone. Chamberlain seemed to wear this visible evidence of his Civil War service proudly. The fractured face was Sam's emblem of heroism, for which he received a special commendation for "gallantry in action" from his commanding officer, Gen. W. W. Averell, and the commanding general of the Army of the Potomac, Gen. Joseph Hooker.

All around the edges of the scrapbook the paintings were "framed" with numerous clippings of pictures from the illustrated magazines of the day like *Harper's Weekly, Frank Leslie's Illustrated Weekly, The Illustrated London News,* and even some prints from books about both the Mexican and Civil wars, along with a number of cartoons. Many of these cutout pictures date from as late as 1903 and possibly served as figure or compositional models for Sam while he was more carefully composing his pictures from his early field sketches. One startling find is a hitherto unknown chromolithograph of Capt. U. S. Grant and his men hauling a howitzer into the bell tower of the church at San Cosme opposite the San Cosme Gate into Mexico City—the first gate to be breached by the U.S. troops in the last battle of the Mexican War. The chromolithograph is by the famous artist Emmanuel Leutze, who is best known for his huge painting, *Washington Crossing the Delaware.*[66]

The elaborate context of the San Jacinto paintings is important not only in dating them but also in interpreting them, especially as they relate to his better-known work, *My Confession.* In a letter of July 3, 1956, to Mrs. D. W. Knepper, then director of the San Jacinto Museum, the late Harry Shaw Newman, revered proprietor of the Old Print Shop in New York City, declared that the "140" watercolors by Samuel Chamberlain were "the earliest ones he made, some of them actually during the years 1846 and 7 and which he later elaborated over a period of twenty-five years into the album, items from which will appear in *Life's* presentation."[67] A comparison between these San Jacinto pictures and those included from the Anne S. K. Brown Military Collection indicates that many of the San Jacinto pictures must have indeed been first sketches, probably made on the spot. This makes them all the more valuable because they represent Sam's first impressions, uninfluenced by the work of other artists.

As he became more skillful, it is probable that he set these first sketches aside when he illustrated the manuscript of *My Confession* and when he began work on a second version of his story, for which the more carefully wrought Brown Collection watercolors appear to be intended.

The title page to the San Jacinto scrapbook reads as follows:

1-8. Emmanuel Leutze's "Captain Sam Grant and his men hauling up howitzer into tower of San Cosme Church"

Grant's howitzer blew away San Cosme gate to Mexico City and allowed the first American troops to pour into the city. This chromolithograph by Leutze appears to be unknown to scholars of his work. Its source beyond its appearance in Sam Chamberlain's scrapbook is unknown to the present author.

This Scrap-book began in 1867
Finished March 12th 1905 donated
to
Chamberlain and Lyman Brown
and
Their Children, Children, Children's [sic]
by
its maker S. E. Chamberlain in his 77th year[68]

Significantly, a photo of Chamberlain in old age is also on the title page. Unfortunately neither Lyman nor Chamberlain Brown, who became New York theatrical agents, had any children. Indeed, it appears that Chamberlain and Lyman Brown, of 145 West Forty-fifth Street, sold the present album to Mr. R. E. Townsend of Annapolis, Maryland, from whom the Old Print Shop and then the San Jacinto Museum acquired it. Lyman Brown apparently sold the illuminated masterpiece, *My Confession,* to the Old Print Shop in 1956, just after Chamberlain Brown died.[69] How he obtained *both* the scrapbook and *My Confession* is in part a mystery, because family tradition has it that Sam had made three books, one for each of his daughters: Tranceita Maria, wife of Dr. James A. Latimer of Cambridge, Massachusetts; Delorious Trevino, wife of George Brown of Hartford, Connecticut; and Carmeleita Hampton, wife of George Irwin Pevear of Boston, Massachusetts.[70] The mystery is partially clarified by the news that Sam's widow spent the last years of her life living with the Browns, who had moved to Cambridge, Massachusetts.[71] She must have had the manuscript of *My Confession,* while the San Jacinto volume also passed down through the Brown family along with whatever else Mary Chamberlain possessed. However, thirteen paintings are in the Anne S. K. Brown Military Collection at Brown University and eight more are owned by Mrs. George S. Dameral of Portland, Maine, Carmeleita's granddaughter. The whereabouts of Sam's other literary and artistic remains and their provenance, as well as the dates of their production by Sam, represent a mystery almost as intriguing as the question of their authenticity. Readers will note the definite difference between many of the pictures in this album and those added from the Anne S. K. Brown Military Collection. The latter, all of which have writing on the back, may well have been part of or intended to be part of the long-rumored "third album" or manuscript story. Or they might have been sketches and drafts for *My Confession,* which was, according to Col. Frederick Todd, the director of the West Point Museum, "created by General Chamberlain in his older age, but based to some extent on notes and sketches made in the field."[72]

The 147 paintings in the San Jacinto collection are, with few exceptions, all watercolors and pencil (graphite), or watercolor and gouache with heightened daubs of white which highlight explosions, cannon fire, clouds and the like. One exception appears on the back of no. 76. It is a pencil drawing of General

"Beauty and the Beast"

1-9. Sam Rescues a Damsel in Distress [Beauty and the Beast]
Watercolor, 5¼ x 7¾ inches

One of Sam's favorite set pieces involved his rescuing buxom young beauties from fates worse than death. In this picture the evil "El Tuerto," with a whip in his right hand, is preparing to flog his beautiful young wife for running away on their wedding day. Sam, who just happened to be passing by, rushes in and comes to the aid of the lovely Carmeleita, whom he found irresistible: "I told her I would take her with me to Camp, that I love [*sic*] her very much, and she should be my 'alma,' my 'dulcy' [*sic*], my 'espousa' [*sic*]. She threw her arms around my neck and sobed [*sic*] like a child for joy." See illustration no. 132 for another version of the same scene.

Taylor and a group of dragoons plus one wounded soldier and one dead soldier. We know that Sam Chamberlain was part of Taylor's guard at Buena Vista, and he appears in this picture second from the left, curls and all. This unfinished drawing, like others in this collection, may represent an intermediate stage in the composition of one of his pictures, or it could be a page from his original sketchbook. Indeed, a large number of the paintings in this collection have the look of early sketchbook treatments—for example, pictures no. 30, "Wool's Army at Monclova"; no. 63, a loosely painted sketch of three dragoon officers, one of whom is being pitched over the head of his horse; and no. 32, perhaps a scene of the same officers sitting on rocks under a tree. The most intriguing of these is illustration no. 146, "Tucson Arizona, 1848," a tiny, very sketchy watercolor, 3¼ by 5⅞ inches, that Sam declared he painted while handcuffed by order of Maj. Lawrence P. Graham.[73] Other peculiarities to notice include no. 140, "Palace of San Idelfonso from a Old Painting in Monte Morelas." It illustrates a story told him, he says, by an old Dominican padre who described Tuloc priests atop an Aztec pyramid platform addressing a crowd of Tuloc onlookers while preparing to sacrifice a Roman Catholic priest—i.e., himself. In fact, the Tuloc priests are holding up what could be other victims' hearts, while behind them the padre kneels at the foot of a hideous idol. In the background, sacrificial smoke rises in a large cloud fading off to the left of the picture. Perhaps Sam was fascinated by the picture, which he saw in Monte Morelos, because it contrasted peaceful, settled Catholic Spain with the barbarism of Aztec Mexico so recently described by the historian William Hickling Prescott in his *The Conquest of Mexico*. Or perhaps he copied it because he heard the legend of how Imanuel the "convert" Tuloc architect destroyed the great cathedral that he designed for the Spaniards and retreated to this traditional pyramid temple. This represents one of Sam's strangest Gothic stories.[74]

Other anomalies in the collection include views of U.S. soldiers at Molino del Rey (see no. 122), several views of the battle for Mexico City, and the multiple hanging of the San Patricio Battalion just as Chapultepec Castle was captured. These are anomalies because we *know* that Sam was not present. Neither was he in the battle for Monterrey, which he claimed to be in the original manuscript of *My Confession* and detailed action scenes of which appear in the Brown Collection, while the San Jacinto collection appears to feature Sam in Monterrey *after* the battle was over. Interestingly enough, some of Chamberlain's most vivid writing in *My Confession* appears in his account of his participation in the Battle of Monterrey. He also includes in the San Jacinto collection several paintings of the Texas Rangers in the fierce fighting for the strategic Bishop's Palace at Monterrey (see nos. 14, 15). Moreover, his two pictures of the Arkansas volunteers massacring civilians in a cave are painted from a viewpoint *within* the cave while the massacre was taking place, a position Sam could not possibly have occupied at the time.

These and other "stretchers" in the San Jacinto collection underscore that the pictures are often redrawn "recollections," as Sam himself proudly admitted. The album is a combination of field sketches, drafts, and finished drawings, including some "recollections" of Scott's campaign, in which Sam did not participate. Its principal interest lies in the fact that it contains some of Sam's earliest work, done in Mexico during his days of wartime adventure, as well as a number of later conjectural scenes, possibly drawn from Mexican War veterans' tales or inspired by popular images from the flood of newspaper, magazine, and book accounts of the war. The album seems to have been intended as a sort of informal history of the whole Mexican War, or a "romance" of the war with Sam as hero.

The San Jacinto album and its relationship to *My Confession* have been the subject of much speculation over the years. Among the unanswered questions, which are mostly important to scholar-detectives in search of absolute accuracy, several merit mention: Did Sam write *My Confession* between 1855 and 1861, drop his pen and watercolors in mid-sentence to rush off to the Civil War, and never return to the memoir, as Roger Butterfield and others believe? Were many of the San Jacinto pictures painted before the aging Sam, despite his growing paralysis from old war wounds, ever undertook the relatively polished and exquisitely illustrated *My Confession*, as Harry Shaw Newman declared? (This seems unlikely, although a newspaper account of the celebration of his eightieth birthday in 1907 indicates that he was by no means totally decrepit.[75]) Or did Sam compose *My Confession* and the paintings in the San Jacinto collection at the same time? On the back of many of the San Jacinto pictures are drafts of his *My Confession* narrative and even a bit of his Arizona adventures. Some of these have extraordinarily well-wrought, uncolored illustrations, one of which is reproduced here, and the handwriting on some of the pages is not Sam's. Did he have a scribe or scribes, perhaps even Wethersfield prison trustees? Did a person or persons unknown redo the sketches from this early draft for the final version of *My Confession*? For the most part the pages are lined watercolor paper, but he also used small blue square sheets resembling personal stationery, as well as newspapers and an equipment-return form from the Civil War (this last would seem to disprove Butterfield's thesis that Sam abandoned *My Confession* after 1861). Did Sam return to *My Confession* when he got a job as prison warden, long after the Civil War, and then assemble the drafts and leftover pictures into the San Jacinto album? The San Jacinto collection would thus represent his last project, containing a range of his artistic and literary endeavors over thirty-seven years.

Sam Chamberlain's San Jacinto scrapbook may remain something of a mystery, but it is also a grand drama, a theater not unlike the Old National of Boston, featuring Sam's recollections of some of the best years of his life, when he came to manhood as a soldier and a lover in Texas and Old Mexico. His memorable Texas views of Rangers and Comanches are not only colorful but full of life. Illustration no. 100, with Sam's dueling opponent stiffly falling, is pure

"El Guerra al Cuchillo."

i-10. "El Guerra [*sic*] at Cuchillo"
Pencil, watercolor and wash, 5⅝ x 7⅝ inches

Sam finds Antonio in bed with his paramours, Nina and Rosita. Scene shows Sam dueling with Antonio while Nina and Rosita cheer Antonio on. For sequel to story see caption for picture 42. Courtesy Anne S. K. Brown Military Collection, Brown University.

theater, as is his portrayal of fierce, leather-clad Mexican guerillas as stage villains. Sam's amorous but dangerous adventures with the two Velasco sisters, which resulted in his betrayal and a deadly duel with the villainous Antonio in their bedroom, are also pure theater. Huddled in bed under a huge crucifix, Sam's former paramours, the sisters Nina and Rosita, cheered Antonio on with cries of "Bravo! Bravo!" "Good Antonio kill kill the big fool," and, better yet, "Antonio, my love, stick the foreigner and come to bed!" Nothing daunted, of course, Sam "gave him a point in a part that made him howl with agony, and would cause him to lose the regards of the 'dos margaritas.'"[76] This is an inspired example of the sort of betrayal melodrama fashionable in Sam's era.

In fact, *My Confession* incorporates all of the conventions of the romance novel; it is a strong historical narrative, like the works of Walter Scott, William H. Ainsworth, G. P. R. James, and other popular writers of the day whom Sam admired, and it links the ancient Mexican past with the present, a technique that also occurred to William Hickling Prescott, the leading historian of the day. Perhaps Sam was trying to write an illustrated romance based on his exploits. He evokes the Gothic novel in his strange stories of decaying cathedrals and deserted ranchos, as well as his tales of Aztecs, devils, and Irish dervishes. He also makes use of the rogue genre, portraying himself as well as the guerrillas as fashionable "banditti" characters like those in Cooper's *The Bravo*. At times Sam even mixes the Gothic and rogue genres with a kind of sly pornography, as in his assertion that a captured sixteen-year-old girl was made to sit naked on the bandit Antonio Canales's banquet table after Canales captured a U.S. supply train. (Other sources indicate that the girl was immediately released, given money, and sent to the nearest town.) In the case of El Tuerto and Carmeleita, Sam includes a pornography of violence comparable to the works of the popular but infamous Lippard, whose *Monks of Monks Hall* was not only a best-seller but a landmark in this genre.[77] Similarly worthy of fiction is his rescue of the Traveina sisters, Maria Tranceita and Delorious, from a fate worse than death at the hands of some wild members of the Second Mississippi Rifles. And then there was the lovely Carmeleita, whom Sam also saves, loves, and lives with as man and wife. There are at least four pictures of Carmeleita in this collection. No wonder he named his daughter after her!

Sam also caught the music and rhythms of the fandango and the more ominous booming, crackling, clashing dances with death in battle, as in his picture of the capture of the gallant O'Brien's guns (nos. 80, 81) or the massacre of an American supply train near Ramos (nos. 119, 120), which he had not seen but had heard described by a survivor. These are only examples of the kinds of illustrations in this collection that are so full of zest or emotion that they do indeed duplicate theater or one of the grand panoramas that unfolded across the stages of the day. Clearly, Sam did not stand in with the Mexican troops who captured O'Brien's guns at Buena Vista, nor did he form with the Mississippi Rifles "the jaws of death," into which the glittering Mexican cavalry charged and were slaughtered; but because he remembered and, in imagination, reconstructed these events better than anyone else, we, his viewers, are there in the thick of the battle. Like much "documentary" art, these pictures may not always qualify as true history, but they have the "feel" or sense of truth; of battles and duels, of fandangos and trysts with señoritas, as well as poetic views of Old Mexico, its towns, cities, cathedrals, ranchos, broad plateaus, mountains, and fearsome passes through these mountains. We know that for the most part Sam Chamberlain was there, but we also travel beyond mere fact into his dreams and fantasies in these captivating paintings that could accurately be termed "romantic," even "surreal," as well as documentary art.

1-11. Sam Chamberlain in old age, circa 1907

NOTES

[1] Samuel Chamberlain, *My Confession: The Recollections of a Rogue, Written and Illustrated by Samuel E. Chamberlain*, ed. with introduction and postscript by Roger Butterfield (New York: Harper and Brothers, 1956). It should be noted that Butterfield took great liberties with Chamberlain's manuscript. He excised roughly one-third of it, eliminated sentences, switched paragraphs, and changed dates (e.g., Sam states that he left San Antonio on August 26, which Butterfield changed to September 25, the correct date, to make Sam's story plausible), as well as corrected Chamberlain's spelling in most but not all cases (e.g., guerrilla still was spelled, in Sam's inimitable fashion, "guerillars"). But then, on page 56, Butterfield says that "in the interest of clarity the publishers have accordingly omitted several pages." This does not clarify but obscures the fact that Sam lied about being a participant in the Battle of Monterrey.

The Butterfield edition has most recently (1987) been reprinted by the University of Nebraska Press in a new paperback edition, without colored illustrations, but with an introduction by John Eisenhower.

At the present time a team of scholars, led by the present author, is working on the original manuscript in an attempt to restore and explain the text as Sam Chamberlain wrote it. Since its partial publication in 1956, however, critical pages are missing from the original manuscript.

[2] L. R. Bryan, Jr., to the Members of the Board of Trustees, San Jacinto Museum of History Association, Nov. 6, 1956, San Jacinto Museum Archives.

Professor Webb and *The Saturday Review* did not back down in the face of Butterfield's threats. Webb's review, "The Memories of a Rogue," appeared on November 3, 1956. In it Webb declared, "Though the author may not have intended a hoax, he has apparently fooled the editor, Roger Butterfield, who states that the manuscript 'remained in obscurity for nearly one hundred years.' Later he says 'Apparently the manuscript was all written between the years 1855 and 1861.'" Webb went on to say, "I have a theory that Sam Chamberlain worked on this manuscript almost until the end of his life, and I know he did so until 1903." Webb's evidence for the 1903 date is the publication of J. M Barrie's play *The Admirable Crichton* in 1903. Chamberlain mentions the character in *My Confession;* thus Webb claims that it establishes the late work on the manuscript.

Webb's comments bear on the present collection in several ways. Though *The Admirable Crichton* as a play was published in 1903, "the Admirable Crichton" is a folk character common to British literature in the eighteenth century and had wide currency in the nineteenth century (see George J. Worth, *William Harrison Ainsworth* [New York: Twayne, 1972], p. 19 and passim). William Harrison Ainsworth published a romance, *Crichton*, in 1837 and, according to Worth, it "had an enormous sale." Ainsworth was considered a romancer like Sir Walter Scott. Chamberlain loved Scott's novels. Perhaps *Crichton* was always one of Sam's favorite books. On the other hand, we know that Chamberlain worked on this San Jacinto album as late as 1905. He says on the title page, "This Scrap-book began in 1867, Finished March 12th, 1905." Thus at least part of Webb's suspicions are correct, but he may have actually been referring to Sam's work on the San Jacinto scrapbook and one other made for the descendants of his third daughter and since broken up into single pictures that come on the market from time to time.

Further, however, Butterfield's statement that the "manuscript [or scripts] remained in obscurity for nearly one hundred years" is in some measure correct. Sam did not publish it, and it did not surface until 1941 in a Hartford antique shop, and then again in 1948, when Sam's grandsons, Lyman and Chamberlain Brown, sold it to a collector, R. E. Townsend. When his brother Chamberlain Brown died in 1955, Lyman Brown put the present San Jacinto collection on the market. Sam, however, did apparently show his manuscript illustrated book to visitors to his home in Barre, Massachusetts. For the most part, though, it and the San Jacinto album remained, if not a family secret, certainly a private writing much in the fashion of *The Education of Henry Adams* or Melville's unpublished *Billy Budd*. As indicated in this introduction, scholars are still at work trying to determine when Chamberlain actually wrote *My Confession,* but there is no ambiguity as to the date of composition of the San Jacinto album.

[3] See footnote above. The Old Print Shop, however, described them as 140 watercolors when there are actually 147, including two duplicates, in the album.

In addition to these pictures, two other odd lots of Sam's paintings and verso writing drafts have been uncovered as a result of this project. Eight of these belong to his great-granddaughter, Mrs. George Dameral of Portland, Maine, former wife of Col. Frederick Todd, former director of the West Point Museum. Thirteen more pictures and verso writings are in the Todd folders in the Anne S. K. Brown Military Collection at Brown University.

In part to fill in Sam's story, but more important for the sake of comparison with the San Jacinto pictures, we have added a number of the Brown Collection pictures to this book (see captions). The Brown Collection pictures, as well as those of Mrs. Dameral, appear to be much more finished and artistic than many of the San Jacinto pictures. One uncolored drawing and manuscript page, which we have included in the introduction, clearly demonstrates Sam's extraordinary skill with pen and ink.

The existence of these two sets of pictures, plus one picture recently acquired by the Summerlee Foundation, may yet add credence to the family stories that Chamberlain did indeed make three albums for his daughters.

[4] *My Confession*, ms. p. 42; University of Nebraska Press edition (hereafter N.E.), p. 40.

[5] Walt Whitman, "So Long," in *Leaves of Grass*, "Songs of Parting" (Boston: Thayer and Eldridge, 1860). For a more accessible version see John Kowenhoven (ed.), Walt Whitman, *Leaves of Grass* (New York: Random House, Modern Library Edition, 1950), 389.

[6] President Polk announced the discovery of gold in California in a message to Congress on December 5, 1848, less than a year after the signing of the Treaty of Guadalupe Hidalgo. The news of the discovery and a gold nugget now in the Smithsonian Institute were brought in a dash across the continent by Navy Lt. Edward Fitzgerald Beale. He arrived in Washington in September 1848.

[7] *My Confession*, ms. p. 148; N.E. pp. 69–70.

[8] Ibid.

[9] William S. McFeely, *Grant: A Biography* (New York: W. W. Norton, 1981), 30. Also see U. S. Grant, *Personal Memoirs of U. S. Grant* (2 vols.; New York: Charles L. Webster and Company, 1885), I, 53. There he also wrote "to this day [I] regard the war, which resulted as one of the most unjust ever waged by a stronger against a weaker nation." For his Whig family background, see Lloyd Lewis, *Captain Sam Grant* (Boston: Little, Brown and Co., 1950), 45–46.

[10] Justin Smith, *The War with Mexico* (2 vols.; New York: Macmillan, 1919), I, 385–386.

[11] *My Confession*, ms. p. 102. Not in N.E.

[12] See Nicholas P. Trist Papers, Library of Congress.

[13] Karl J. Bauer, *The Mexican War, 1846–1848*, pp. 396–397, compares the situation to that of the U.S. in the Vietnam War..

[14] *My Confession*, ms. p. 102. Not in N.E.

[15] Eisenhower, "Foreword," *My Confession*, N.E., p. xii.

[16] Ibid.

[17] "Veteran of Two Wars," obituary, West Point Museum.

[18] *My Confession*, ms. pp. 1, 3; N.E., pp. 7, 9.

[19] Ibid., ms. p. 3; N.E., p. 9.

[20] Ibid., ms. p. 22; N.E., p. 25.

[21] Ibid.

[22] Ibid., ms. p. 27; N.E. pp. 28–29.

[23] Mark Twain, *Adventures of Huckleberry Finn* (New York: Charles L. Webster Co., 1885), 1.

[24] *My Confession*, ms. pp. 28–34. Not in N.E.

[25] "Doughboy" seems to derive specifically from the Texas Rangers making bread during their campaign. Sam especially notes this in his description of the aftermath of the capure of the Bishop's Palace at Monterrey, but it must have been common practice among the volunteer infantry before this, because Sam uses the term early on in his narrative. Some have said it stems from infantrymen having to apply clay whitener to their white crisscrossing belts. Sam might have been ironically comparing the bread-making of the Texans to the clay-making of the regular infantry.

[26] Enlistment paper, U.S. Pension Office Records, Sept. 8, 1846, National Archives. Sam called the Chief Justice of Bexar "the Alcalde" because he also served as unofficial mayor.

[27] *My Confession*, ms. p. 43; N.E., p. 41.

[28] Ibid., ms. p. 44; N.E. p. 41.

[29] Ibid.

[30] Ibid., ms. p. 49; N.E. p. 43.

[31] Sam's detailed Mexican War service record does not exist, but in a long letter in the Washington *Union* of February 9, 1847, Lieutenant Carleton makes clear that he was with Wool's army all the way and not in the Battle of Monterrey.

[32] Eisenhower, "Foreword," *My Confession*, N.E., p. xii. For Taylor's real instructions to Captain Bragg, see Bauer, *The Mexican War, 1846–1848*, 216. What Taylor actually said was, "Well double-shot your guns and give 'em hell, Bragg."

[33] *My Confession*, ms. p. 167; N.E. pp. 133–134.

This information concerning the New Orleans *Daily Delta* articles of June 16 and July 19, 1847, was supplied by Thomas Kailbourn, to whom thanks are due.

[34] Justin Smith, quoted in Eisenhower, "Foreword," *My Confession*, N.E., p. xv.

[35] Henry F. Dobyns (ed.), *Hepah California! The Journal of Cave Johnson Couts...* (Tucson: Arizona Pioneers Historical Society, 1961), 48, fn. 27.

[36] *My Confession*, ms. p. 373; N.E. pp. 290–291.

[37] Ibid., ms. pp. 371–373; N.E. pp. 290–297. For a more complete but undocumented account, see Douglas G. Martin, *Yuma Crossing* (Albuquerque: University of New Mexico Press, 1954), 138–149. But see note 41 below for another participant's account.

[38] Samuel Chamberlain, "Three Months Campaign of the First Volunteer Company in the United States For the War," ms., West Point Museum, p. 1. Also see Chamberlain Society printing of a banquet given by the First Volunteers Citizens Association, April 29, 1909, commemorating Chamberlain, p. 36, West Point Museum.

[39] *Daily Alta California,* Oct. 10–20, 1854.

[40] See note 35 above.

[41] Andrew Hays Cargill, "C. O. Brown's story of the Lincoln Massacre at Fort Yuma in 1850," ms., May 1907, Arizona Historical Society, Tucson, Arizona. See especially pp. 15–18. C. O. Brown was a member of the Glanton Gang that had destroyed the Yuma ferry and Dr. Lincoln's ferry. Most of them paid for it with their lives, but several gang members, including Chamberlain, Fillipe Valenzuela, and Brown, escaped to California.

Brown carried with him $2,000, but he knew that Glanton, fearing an Indian raid, had deposited $7,000 in a San Diego bank and buried $45,000 in gold dollars in a large jar under a mesquite tree (p. 15). In 1857, Brown returned to the Yuma site only to find U.S. military officers camped on the very spot where the treasure was buried. Knowing that if he told the soldiers about the treasure they would confiscate it, he put off the "dig" and went to work in Tucson. When he returned to the Yuma crossing the mesquite tree had disappeared and the U.S. Indian agent, now in charge of the region, refused him permission to prospect for the treasure on what was by then Yuma Reservation land. Cargill told this story as late as 1907. Perhaps the treasure is still there.

[42] "Hidden Treasures: Arms from All Parts of the World in Gen. Chamberlain's 'Den' at Barre Plains," clipping from Ware (Mass.) *River News,* Mar. 5, 1896, West Point Museum.

[43] Chamberlain biography in *Worster County,* photocopy at West Point. The family tradition concerning Sam's meeting with his future wife is from an interview with his great-granddaughter, Mrs. George S. Dameral, of Portland, Maine.

[44] Thomas Wentworth Higginson, *Massachusetts in the Army and Navy During the War of 1861–65* (Boston: Wright and Potter Printing Co., State Printers, 1896), 158, 166–167. James L. Bowen, *Massachusetts in the War, 1861–65* (Springfield, Mass.: C. W. Bryan & Co., 1889), 136–137. Butterfield, p. 300. Also see Bliss Perry (ed.), *The Life and Letters of Henry Lee Higginson* (Boston: Atlantic Monthly Press, 1921), 218, fn. 1. He was also referred to as a "bacon smoker," possibly slang for fireman.

[45] Maj. Gen. William A. Bancroft, M.V.M. (Ret.), Late Brigadier-General, U.S. Vols., "Brevet Brigadier-General Samuel E. Chamberlain, U.S. Vols.," published by The Chamberlain Association of America (Boston, 1909), West Point Museum, p. 37.

[46] The ms. map and a description of the battle by Harry W. Littlefield, Late 2nd Lt., Acting Adjt. 1st Massachusetts Cavalry, are in the West Point Museum.

[47] Bowen, *Massachusetts in the War, 1861–65,* 899.

[48] *Worster County,* 305.

[49] Ibid., 305. Also see Chamberlain Pension Records, National Archives.

[50] At this time, Charles Francis Adams II withdrew from the First Massachusetts and was given a cavalry squadron of his own. It seems clear that he did not want to serve under either Horace B. Sargent or Sam Chamberlain. He wrote to Henry Lee Higginson, "A lower-toned, more vulgar regiment than ours [the First Massachusetts] I never saw and the deterioration since I left it in Jany. is to me amazing. . . . Will Chamberlain succeed in reforming this? I don't know. . . ."

By September, Colonel Chamberlain wrote to Higginson echoing Adams: "The last month's campaign exceeds in severity all the previous ones, and we must have rest. . . . I cannot imagine what has come over the North, what has brought about this strong apathy and criminal carelessness about filling up the army. We want men, not a lot of sickly Boys [sic] and cripples, where is all the boasted patriotism of Massachusetts gone too [sic], to have her send agents to collect sick scum and trash, that has been sent in of late."

The snobbish Adams revised his opinion of Chamberlain in his *Autobiography*: "Only once do I remember going back to the regiment. Chamberlain was then in command. A large, rough, self-made man, he had been wild and adventurous in his youth serving as a trooper in the Mexican war. Wholly lacking in refinement and education, he was a dashing fellow in his way; and on the whole, I fancy, the best officer that regiment ever had. . . . Chamberlain and I then parted good friends, and afterwards remained such." Perry (ed.), *Life and Letters of Henry Lee Higginson,* 218, 230. Also Charles Francis Adams II, *Charles Francis Adams, 1835–1915: An Autobiography* (Boston and New York: Houghton Mifflin Co., The Riverside Press, Cambridge, 1916), 155.

[51] *Massachusetts in the War,* p. 899; Benjamin W. Crowninshield, *A History of the First Regiment of Massachusetts Cavalry Volunteers* (Boston: Houghton-Mifflin Co., 1891), 240. Also see Chamberlain's

service record in the National Archives. Special thanks to Judge David A. Jackson, who researched Chamberlain's Civil War career in the *Official Records of the War of the Rebellion.*

[52] Crowninshield, 240.

[53] Higginson, 166.

[54] John Salmon Ford, *Rip Ford's Texas,* ed. Stephen B. Oates (Austin: University of Texas Press, 1987), 388–396.

[55] Higginson, 166.

[56] *Worster County,* 305; *Massachusetts in the War,* 899.

[57] Bancroft, *Chamberlain Association,* 38.

[58] Hartford *Courant,* June 22, 1893. Note, however, that Chamberlain retired just after this exoneration.

[59] Ibid., Feb. 18, 1889.

[60] Ms. postcard, Connecticut State Library, Hartford, Connecticut.

[61] See for example the Boston *Herald,* Jan. 30, 1906, which featured a drawing of General Chamberlain holding forth at a reception for military veterans hosted by Governor Guild. West Point Museum.

[62] Pension Records, Interior Department, Jan. 22, 1906, National Archives. Also see 59th Cong., 1st Sess., Senate Report No. 372.

[63] See obituaries, West Point Museum. He was eighty years, eleven months, and ten days old.

[64] Ibid. The poet appears to be M. J. Hottery.

[65] Archibald Clavering Gunter, ms., New York, March 25, 1903, West Point Museum. This was in reply to Chamberlain's letter of March 23, 1903. Gunter, a Liverpudlian by birth and reared in California, finally became a New York broker and publisher. He was also a successful playwright and best-selling novelist. The book about which he wrote Sam was *The Spy Company* (1903). The reviewer for the *Saturday Review* of August 22, 1903, wrote that "a schoolboy would pronounce this 'a rattling good story' . . . this tale of the Mexican War rattles along to the accompaniment of cracking revolvers, yelling Comanches, the thud of mustang hooves and the 'Waughs' . . . of Texan scouts." The reviewer for the staid British *Atheneum* of June 20, 1903, wrote, "This is a tale of the Mexican War for the annexation of Texas. . . . Though there is little pretension to style about it, the author can pile on innumerable incidents and Texan rangers, Mexican rancheros and bandits, wild men of all sorts, white, yellow and red, skirmish, to the raising, at any rate, of the reader's hair."

[66] See Chamberlain Scrapbook, San Jacinto Museum.

[67] Harry Shaw Newman to Mrs. David W. Knepper, Director, San Jacinto Museum Association, July 3, 1956, San Jacinto Museum Archives.

[68] Chamberlain Scrapbook, San Jacinto Museum.

[69] L. R. Bryan, Jr., to the Members of the Board of Trustees, San Jacinto Museum of History Association, Nov. 16, 1956, San Jacinto Museum Archives.

Mr. R. E. Townsend related to Mr. Bryan an intriguing tale of the fate of Sam Chamberlain's *My Confession* and two other Chamberlain scrapbooks. Townsend declared that he "first discovered the Chamberlain book with an antique dealer in Hartford, Connecticut in 1941." He also recalled seeing a scrapbook, different from that being sold by the Old Print Shop. This scrapbook consisted of "signed original orders and documents" and no pictures. Later, in 1948, he located the Brown brothers in New York and purchased *My Confession* from them. It is apparent from this account that the Brown brothers never really valued their grandfather's Mexican War masterpiece. Mr. Townsend and Roger Butterfield both added that Lyman Brown "is an eccentric character to say the least."

[70] Interview with Mrs. George S. Dameral, 1992.

[71] Mary Chamberlain obituary, West Point Museum.

[72] Col. Frederick Todd notebooks, Vol. I, Anne S. K. Brown Military Collection, Brown University.

Colonel Todd adds: "Apparently General Chamberlain worked on a second and almost duplicate copy of the journal; it is not known whether it was completed or not. At some time, illustrations were cut out of this copy and the compiler's wife (a great granddaughter of the General) [Mrs. George Dameral] procured these in 1941 for the compiler's father, a book dealer, who sold them to A. M. Craighead [an Ohio dealer]. When the Craighead art collection came to the West Point Museum in 1968 [*sic:* It was 1957] it presented this small group of watercolors to the compiler and these are also in this album [i.e., the Todd notebook]."

[73] *My Confession,* ms. p. 334; N.E. p. 258.

[74] Ibid., ms. pp. 372–383. Not in N.E.

[75] "Mexican War Veteran Celebrates His Birthday" (1907), West Point Museum. The reporter wrote, "comparatively few are permitted to pass beyond the four score mark and still enjoy all their faculties. But for one who has passed through so much in this life as the subject of this sketch, it is much more remarkable."

[76] *My Confession*, ms. p. 107; N.E. p. 73.

[77] All of these genres add up to the typical romance novel as well as pure and not-so-pure melodrama. The literary influences on Sam were striking. Robert W. Johannsen in *To the Halls of the Montezumas: The Mexican War in the American Imagination* (New York: Oxford University Press, 1985) treats this subject in fascinating scope and detail. He points out that a veritable flood of books, plays, prints, histories, autobiographies, and geographies resulted from the Mexican War in the years 1847 to around 1855. These ranged from serious works to dime novels. They often incorporated virtual copies of the chivalric romances of Scott and G. P. R. James. In fact, their emphases on individual chivalry and collective patriotism were often deliberately set against "progress" and "money getting." Heroes abounded; at one time Scott, Taylor, Worth, and Capt. (later Lt. Col.) Charley May were characterized as "American Murats," in reference to one of Napoleon's greatest marshals. Indeed, references to Napoleon as the epitome of the chivalric hero abounded; even Santa Anna saw himself as "the Napoleon of the West." War and chivalry, in these books and in this romantic age, were deemed necessary to a civilization. So, too, were visions of exotic foreign lands that evoked "the mystic chords of memory." Histories in this spirit were turned out by the hundreds, though Prescott, the grandest historian of the day, whose *Conquest of Mexico* (1844) cried out for a modern parallel, declined to write one, since he abhorred the war and writing about still-living characters. It was left to lesser writers like Thomas Bangs Thorpe, George C. Furber, Brantz Mayer, John Frost, and George Wilkins Kendall of the New Orleans *Picayune* to write lesser histories. Kendall's, in fact, lies unpublished in the Barker Texas History Center at the University of Texas.

Melodramas on stage abounded and were supplemented by giant unfolding stage panoramas of the war, complete with fireworks and the sound of guns. Musicians chipped in with such favorites as *Captain May's Quickstep* and Stephen Foster's haunting *Santa Anna's Retreat from Buena Vista*. Another favorite was *Santa Anna's Wooden Leg*. Meanwhile, the art of lithography was propelled forward in giant steps as Nathaniel Currier led the way with no less than eighty-five prints of the war, some reeking of sentiment, others pictures of bloody clashes. They reified romance and melodramatic thoughts, and Currier's depictions of mountains appear to be clear models for Chamberlain's brush and pencil. It is almost as if Currier and, at times, official army artist Daniel P. Whiting supplied the scenic backdrops for Sam's melodramatic adventures.

The romance novel is very clearly dissected in George J. Worth, *William Harrison Ainsworth* (New York: Twayne Publishers, 1972).

SUGGESTIONS FOR FURTHER READING:

THE MOST accessible account of Sam Chamberlain's adventures is the abridged edition: Samuel E. Chamberlain, *My Confession, The Recollections of a Rogue,* introduction and postscript by Roger Butterfield; foreword by John Eisenhower (Lincoln: University of Nebraska Press, 1987).

For anyone interested in the Mexican-American War per se, the best place to start is Norman E. Tutorow (comp. and ed.), *The Mexican-American War: An Annotated Bibliography* (Westport, Conn.: Greenwood Press, 1981).

There exist numerous histories of the Mexican War. The most comprehensive of these, because he was able to interview veterans, including Sam Chamberlain, is Justin Smith, *The War with Mexico* (2 vols.; New York: Macmillan, 1919).

The most comprehensive contemporary history is Lt. Roswell S. Ripley, *The War with Mexico* (2 vols.; 1849; reprint, New York: Burt Franklin, 1970). This work is based primarily on published reports by the field commanders in the U.S. House and Senate Documents Series. See also Nathan Covington Brooks, *A Complete History of the Mexican War, 1846–1848* (1849; Chicago: Rio Grande Press, 1965), reprinted with an introduction by Gilberto Espinosa.

Two other works that approach the war from unusual angles and are especially impressive are Robert W. Johannsen, *To the Halls of the Montezumas: The Mexican War in the American Imagination* (New York: Oxford University Press, 1985) and Martha A. Sandweiss, Rick Stewart, and Ben W. Huseman, *Eyewitness to War: Prints and Daguerreotypes of the Mexican War, 1846–1848* (Fort Worth: Amon Carter Museum; Washington, D.C.: Smithsonian Institution Press, 1989). The latter, a profusely illustrated work, is a sequel to Ronnie C. Tyler, *The Mexican War: A Lithographic Record,* introduction by Stanley Ross (Austin: Texas State Historical Association, 1973).

The two best modern overviews of the war are Karl Jack Bauer, *The Mexican War, 1846–1848* (New York: Macmillan, 1974) and John S. D. Eisenhower, *So Far From God: The U.S. War with Mexico, 1846–1848* (New York: Random House, 1989).

Other useful books related to the war are:

Francis Baylies, *A Narrative of Major General Wool's Campaign in Mexico in the Years 1846, 1847, and 1848* (Albany: Little and Co., 1851).

Alfred Hoyt Bill, *Rehearsal for Conflict* (New York: Alfred A. Knopf, 1947).

Bernard De Voto, *The Year of Decision, 1846* (Boston: Little, Brown and Co., 1943).

Odie Faulk and Joseph Stout (eds.), *The Mexican War, Changing Interpretations* (Chicago: The Swallow Press, 1973).

John Frost, *Pictorial History of Mexico and the Mexican War* (Philadelphia: Cowperthwait, 1849).

William H. Goetzmann, *When the Eagle Screamed: The Romantic Horizon in American Diplomacy, 1800–1860* (New York: John Wiley & Sons, 1966).

Robert Self Henry, *The Story of the Mexican War* (Indianapolis: Bobbs-Merrill & Co., 1950).

David Lavender, *Climax at Buena Vista: The American Campaign in Northeastern Mexico* (Philadelphia: J. B. Lippincott Co., 1966).

Douglas D. Martin, *Yuma Crossing* (Albuquerque: University of New Mexico Press, 1954).

Cormac McCarthy, *Blood Meridian* (New York: Ecco Press, 1985). An extraordinary novel based in large part, according to the author, on Sam Chamberlain's later adventures as related in *My Confession.*

Frederick Merk, *Manifest Destiny and Mission in American History: A Reinterpretation* (New York: Alfred A. Knopf, 1963).

Frederick Merk, *The Monroe Doctrine and American Expansionism, 1843–1846* (New York: Alfred A. Knopf, 1966).

Carl Nebel and George Wilkins Kendall, *War Between the United States and Mexico, Illustrated* (New York: D. Appleton & Co., 1851). Nebel's twelve illustrations for this work are perhaps the outstanding overall battle scenes of the war.

David Nevin, *The Mexican War* (Alexandria, Va.: Time-Life Books, 1978).

Albert C. Ramsey (trans.), *The Other Side: or, Notes for the History of the War Between Mexico and the United States* (New York: John Wiley, 1850).

Samuel C. Reid, Jr., *The Scouting Expeditions of McCulloch's Texas Rangers; or the Summer and Fall Campaigns of the Army of the United States in Mexico—1846* (Philadelphia: J. W. Bradley, 1860).

Theodore F. Rodenbough, *From Everglades to Cañon with the Second Dragoons . . . 1836–1875* (New York: Van Nostrand, 1875).

Otis A. Singletary, *The Mexican War* (Chicago: University of Chicago Press, 1960).

George Winston Smith and Charles Judah (eds.), *Chronicles of the Gringos: The U.S. Army in the Mexican War, 1846–1848, Accounts of Eyewitnesses and Combatants* (Albuquerque: University of New Mexico Press, 1968).

Thomas Bangs Thorpe, *Our Army at Monterrey* (Philadelphia: Carey and Hart, 1847).

Thomas Bangs Thorpe, *Our Army on the Rio Grande* (Philadelphia: Carey and Hart, 1846).

Edward S. Wallace, *General William Jenkins Worth: Monterrey's Forgotten Hero* (Dallas: Southern Methodist University Press, 1953).

THE PAINTINGS

1. ALTON, ILLINOIS
Watercolor and pencil, 1⁵⁄₈ x 5³⁄₄ inches

Gen Wool Addressing the Mutineers

2. GENERAL WOOL ADDRESSING THE MUTINEERS
Watercolor and graphite, 5⅜ x 7⅞ inches

This mutiny, by the Alton Volunteer Guards at Alton, Illinois, was provoked by their drunken commander, whom Sam mistakenly called Captain Goft (there was no Goft or Goff in the Alton Guards). Chamberlain claims to have become captain of "a hundred half drunken desperadoes." Seeing General Wool, several colonels, and Illinois Governor Ford approaching, Sam quickly put down the mutiny and "dressed the ranks" and commanded the men to "present arms." The Alton Guards got off with a reprimand from General Wool, as seen in this picture. Sam appears in front of the ranks without his long, golden locks. He was made the scapegoat of the mutiny and reduced to the ranks by General Wool.

3. MISSION SAN HOSEA [JOSÉ]
Watercolor and graphite, 3¹⁵⁄₁₆ x 5⅛ inches

This is probably Chamberlain's first sketch or painting of San Antonio, Texas.

4. MISSION CONCEPCIÓN, SAN ANTONIO
Pencil drawing, 2⅜ x 5 inches

5. MISSION CONCEPCIÓN, SAN ANTONIO
Pencil drawing with ink wash, 2½ x 8¹⁄₁₆ inches

The dragoon encampment is in the foreground; Mission Concepción is in the background. Note the cloud of bats flying out of the deserted mission. Before the soldiers could occupy it, they had to shovel two feet of bat guano from the floor.

6. Military Plaza and Main Plaza, San Antonio
Watercolor and graphite on thin, light-gray paper, 7 x 12⅛ inches

This portrays the departure of Wool's troops from San Antonio. Sam writes, "The command made quite an imposing appearance as they marched through the Grand Plaza of San Antonio, which was crowded with a motley assembly of wild looking Texans, Mexicans in their everlasting blankets, Negro Slaves, with a sprinkling of Lipan Indians, in full dress of paint and feathers, White women, Squaws and Senoretas [*sic*]." Note, too, that Sam prominently includes the flag of a greatly exaggerated Bexar Exchange saloon, where he had so many adventures with the "wild Texans."

7. SAM MEETS HIS FORMER LOVE KATHERINE AT CASTROVILLE
Watercolor, pencil and light gouache, 3¾ x 7⅛ inches, writing on verso

Upon meeting Katherine, to whom he had been "betrothed," and her stout German husband, Sam exclaimed, "inconstancy thy name art woman." He added, "Her husband was a stupid Dutchman . . . ." The army marched out of the Castroville encampment playing, according to Sam, "The Girl I Left Behind Me." Courtesy Anne S. K. Brown Military Collection, Brown University.

8. Colonel Harney's Dragoons Cross the Rio Grande into Mexico
Watercolor, 5³⁄₈ x 7⁵⁄₈ inches

Colonel Harney's First Dragoons, of which Sam was a member, preceded Wool's main force to scout out a possible Mexican ambush.

9. Matamoros from Fort Brown

Watercolor, 5¼ x 7 inches, very little gouache, mostly transparent

Fort Brown and cannonballs are in the left foreground. At center is the ferry to Matamoros, in the distance. The steamer is the *Col. Taylor.* Another steamer, whose smoke can be seen at the far left, is approaching. One of these boats, the *Col. Cross,* was piloted by Capt. Richard King, later founder of the mammoth King Ranch, which is legendary in Texas. Note: Wool's army crossed the Rio Grande on pontoon boats much farther up the river at Presidio. This picture was undoubtedly drawn when Sam visited friends or was perhaps sent on an errand to Fort Brown. The steamboats signify the strategic importance of the place.

10. Presidio del Rio Grande, Sept. 1846
Watercolor, 3¾ x 7¹/₁₆ inches, no gouache

Note that newspaper upon which this picture may be painted has bled through in the upper right corner. Could this be an original sketch done on the spot? Not likely, because Sam claimed always to carry a sketchbook with him.

THE BATTLE OF MONTERREY

September 21–23, 1846

PLATES 11–23

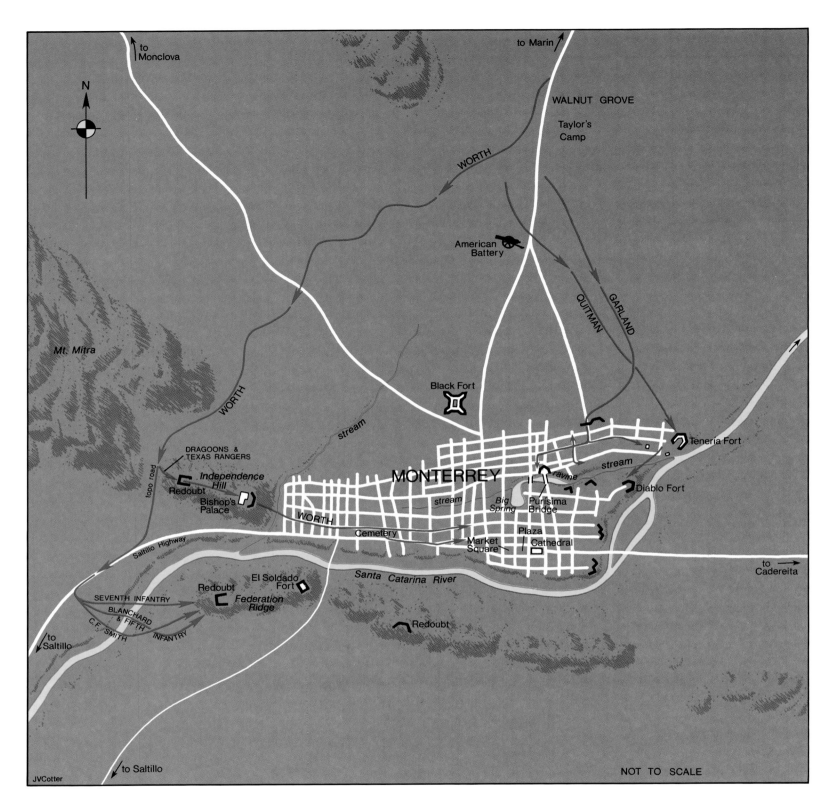

THE BATTLE OF MONTERREY

11. VIEW OF MONTERREY
Watercolor, 4³⁄₈ x 7³⁄₈ inches

Stones in right foreground list strategic fortifications of the city. This must have been painted at a later date, because Sam Chamberlain was not in the Battle of Monterrey. It nevertheless accurately portrays the points of interest in the battle.

Rancho. San Jeromino

12. Skirmish at Rancho San Jeronimo
Watercolor, gouache, 6⅛ x 7¼ inches, writing on verso, gray paper

This is part of the battle for Monterrey. Notice flags and fortresses on Independence Hill, as well as bursts of cannon fire. For a touch of realism, Chamberlain put in "the foul carrion birds" who feasted on the slain soldiers. Sam was not there to witness it, however. Instead, it was the Texas Rangers under Capt. Jack Hays and some of General Worth's regulars who were in this stirring attack.

Capture of the Independence Hill

13. CAPTURE OF INDEPENDENCE HILL
Dark and heavy watercolor, some gouache on yellow paper, 6½ x 7¼ inches, description of attack on verso

The capture of Independence Hill was the key to the battle. It enabled the Americans to fire down on the Bishop's Palace and then the city, to dominate the road to Saltillo, and to climb over the mountain ridge and successfully storm the Bishop's Palace, the other strategic location that dominated the city. The climb up the steep hill on the right slope through cactus and sharp rocks in stormy weather was exceedingly difficult. When the American flag was raised atop the hill, it inspired the troops, and conjures up images of Mt. Surabachi at Iwo Jima to those who remember World War II. Chamberlain accurately portrays the stormy, wet conditions in the "Capture of Independence Hill," even though he was not present.

14. Texas Rangers in Combat in the Courtyard of the Bishop's Palace
Watercolor and gouache on thin, light-gray paper, 6¾ x 12⅜ inches

Sam must have derived this and the previous pictures from accounts told to him by Texas Rangers and other participants. Note, however, the mix of Rangers and U.S. regulars.

15. Desperate Fight Inside the Bishop's Palace
Watercolor and gouache, 5⅜ x 7⅜ inches

The Texas Rangers battling Mexican troops inside the Bishop's Palace stronghold. Other U.S. troops, with flag and cannon dragged up Independence Hill with great difficulty, are arriving through the door at right. The clouds of smoke are from rifle fire. Note how the exaggerated dimensions of the Bishop's Palace make this a surreal scene.

Fight in the "Calle de Iturbide" Church of Sante Maria.

16. Fight in the "Calle de Iturbide," Church of Santa Maria
Watercolor, pencil, gouache, 7⅝ x 6¾ inches, careful writing on back

"We found ourselves in a hornet's nest, every house was a fort." Courtesy Anne S. K. Brown Military Collection, Brown University.

17. CATHEDRAL AT MONTERREY. ARMY RESTING IN FOREGROUND. SAM WALKER'S
TEXANS AT THE SURRENDER OF MONTERREY.

Watercolor, 6⅛ x 7⅜ inches

This is a view of the main plaza at Monterrey from the post office where Sam
Walker's Texans rested at the surrender of Monterrey, which is taking place below in
the plaza. The cathedral does not resemble the still-existing one, nor does it resemble
Stephen G. Hill's lithograph view of 1847. Note surrender flag atop the cathedral on
the side of the mountain in the distance, and the landmark Saddle Mountain. Sam
claims to have been present, but never saw this scene either.

18. SURRENDER OF BLACK FORT, MONTERREY
Watercolor, pencil and gouache, 4½ x 6 inches, writing on verso, also writing on picture surface not covered by paint

The Black Fort, garrisoned by the Fourth Infantry under the command of Col. José Lopez Uraga, here seen surrendering, was perhaps the strongest point in the defense of Monterrey. It was not carried by storming U.S. troops, but was outflanked and surrounded. The Black Fort is medieval in its appearance. It resembles the Alcazar in Seville. Note the portcullis ready to drop down on the gate.

19. INTERIOR OF CATHEDRAL AT MONTERREY
Watercolor 5⁵⁄₁₆ x 7³⁄₄ inches

Note priest holding up host while U.S. dragoons casually ride horses through the church in desecration of it.

20. Sam Sketching Outside Monterrey
Watercolor, gouache, 3 11/16 x 6 7/16 inches, gray paper and writing on verso

This documents the fact that Sam did carry a sketchbook with him on the campaigns, though here he is sketching long after the battle in which he did not participate. He does picture strategic battle points on the left flank of the U.S. attack on Monterrey, such as the Teneria and Purissima Bridge.

21. Saddle Mountain, Monterrey
Watercolor, 2 1/8 x 3 13/16 inches

El Fandango

22. El Fandango

Watercolor, gouache and pencil, 4³/₁₆ x 7 inches

Sam, though wounded in the head, he says, in the struggle for the Bishop's Palace, nonetheless accompanied Lieutenant Carleton on a reconnaissance to the little town of Saleanus (Salinas). There, the ladies of the town got up a fandango. Out of prudence, Lieutenant Carleton forbade his men to attend. Sam, with torn, blood-stained trousers and bandaged head, attended anyway. As wounded hero, he asserted, "I was certainly the Lion of the evening . . . . Shouts of silver toned laughter greeted me and the black eyed beauties were my friends at once." The men, one holding a handkerchief to his nose as if a bad smell had entered, left with "three dozzen [*sic*] Senoras muttering an untranslatable curse, 'carajaho!' [carajo]." Note bandage on Sam's head. Sam is clearly stretching a point here. He was not at the Battle of Monterrey, though he may have been on a scout to Salinas, north of Monterrey. Courtesy Anne S. K. Brown Military Collection, Brown University.

23. ROAD TO SALTILLO, AFTER CAPTURE OF MONTERREY
Watercolor and gouache, 2³⁄₁₆ x 7⁵⁄₈ inches

One can barely see troops marching right to left toward Saltillo.

24. General Wool's Army Marching into Mexico toward Monclova
Watercolor, 6¾ x 12 inches

Sam has this picture sequence out of order. Wool's army, including Sam, marched from Presidio to Monclova and did not take part in the battle for Monterrey. This view, of course, allows Sam to be at two places with two parts of the army at once. The spying Indians behind bushes at right center of picture are an interesting touch. If Sam was with the column, he may or may not have seen the Indians, but he seems to have added Comanche horsemen as a reminder of the precarious existence of North Mexican cities.

25. RUINS OF A CONVENT NEAR MONCLOVA
Watercolor, 4¹³/₁₆ x 5¹³/₁₆ inches

26. MONTECLOVA [*sic*]
Watercolor, ink and pencil, 4¼ x 7⅝ inches

Illustrated start of another chapter, "O'Brien's Story," on verso. Courtesy Anne S. K. Brown Military Collection, Brown University.

27. CHAMBERLAIN'S ENTRY INTO MONCLOVA
Watercolor and pencil, 2⅜ x 4⁵⁄₁₆ inches

Chamberlain writes: "I made my entry into this delightful place lashed to my saddle suffering from an attack of mani-a spotu [*sic*], four days in Hospital brought me around allright [*sic*] and in defiance of my late warning in the dissipation of the place . . . ." This picture is not finished.

The "Man with the Poker"

28. "THE MAN WITH THE POKER"
Watercolor, pencil, gouache, 4³/₁₆ x 7¼ inches. Start of chapter, "O'Brien's Story," with watercolor scene to open verso page.

Sam had been drinking heavily when he went on guard duty. Then a "little old fellow dressed in red stood before me grinning and winking with a pair of eyes that shone like candles." It was "the man with the Poker." Sam fired, "aiming between his confounded bright eyes, but he only winked the harder." Sam had delirium tremens. Courtesy Anne S. K. Brown Military Collection, Brown University.

Montclova with Mexican Market at our Encampment; Dancing Girl, Monte Dealers &c

29. MONTCLOVA [*sic*] WITH MEXICAN MARKET AT OUR ENCAMPMENT; DANCING GIRL,
MONTE DEALERS, ETC.
Watercolor and pencil, 7¼ x 12⅝ inches

General Wool's army, to which Chamberlain was attached, marched directly from
Presidio del Rio Grande to Monclova at approximately the time of the Battle of
Monterrey. This is probably Sam's eyewitness view.

30. WOOL'S ARMY AT MONCLOVA
Watercolor and pencil sketch, 2¾ x 3 inches

This may be one of Sam's original field sketches.

31. IRISH SOLDIER PRESENTING ARMS TO GENERAL WOOL
Watercolor and graphite, 2¹¹⁄₁₆ x 2⁷⁄₁₆ inches, painted over yellow lined paper

The six-foot Irish guard "was bent in the most extraordinary manner, near double," according to Chamberlain. Wool, taken aback, asked what was the matter. The sentry replied, "The General will excuse me but ever since I have ate corn, I have been troubled with a goneness and bastely appetite, and faith I believe I am turning into a horse and will be on all fours before long." A tall tale.

32. THREE DRAGOONS SITTING ON ROCKS TELLING STORIES
Watercolor, 2¾ x 3⅛ inches, thin, light-gray paper, part of a letter on verso

Walnut Springs, just outside Monterrey, was the main campground of Taylor's army. Note the Grimsley saddle with high pommel and cantle, made so the rider would not fall off the horse while asleep. Sam's discriminating eye here proves that he was present with the dragoons.

33. O'Brien Nearly Lets Captive General Escape
Watercolor, graphite and gouache, 3⅜ x 3¾ inches, large writing verso

While guarding a captive general in Spain, O'Brien was confronted in the middle of the night by officers who intended to let his prisoner escape. In the ensuing melee, O'Brien killed his prisoner; for this he was court-martialed and sentenced to death, but escaped in a padre's costume. O'Brien and other old soldiers were swapping tales of many wars in Africa, Asia, India, and the Wild West. O'Brien's story is about his adventures as a soldier of fortune in the Spanish war with France.

34. Mexican Guerrillas
Watercolor, 5½ x 7 inches

In this very colorful picture the guerrillas, whom Sam observed up close from beneath a clump of yuccas, seem intent on a raid on the town below. Note other guerrillas in the left rear of the picture. Sam was terrified of them, especially their "national weapon, the 'Lasso.'" The *escopeta* or short unrifled carbine shown here was so inaccurate that it did not scare anybody.

35. MEXICAN GUERRILLA ON THE LOOKOUT WITH ESCOPETTA [*sic*]
Watercolor and pencil on horizontally lined paper, 4¹⁄₁₆ x 4¹⁄₁₆ inches

This horse, unlike so many others that Sam drew, is awkward, with its small head completely out of proportion.

36. Skirmish at Rio [Arroyo de] Los [*sic*] Palmas
Watercolor, 3⁷⁄₈ x 7³⁄₈ inches

Here Sam pictures a successful attack on a Mexican supply train on the Monclova road. Led by Sgt. Jack Miller of the Second Dragoons, a small American force charged and captured the large supply train in perhaps Sam's most heroic action. "In the attack on the main body [of lancers]," Sam wrote, "I found myself alongside a black whiskered chap who lunged at me with his lance. I parried it and gave him a 'right cut' across the face, which added neither to his beauty or health." Courtesy Anne S. K. Brown Military Collection, Brown University.

Skirmish of Rio Los Palmos.

37. ANOTHER VERSION OF THE "SKIRMISH OF RIO LOS PALMOS [LAS PALMAS]"
Watercolor, 6¼ x 7⁷⁄₁₆ inches

This is a cruder version and probably done by Sam while in Mexico.

38. Paso del Diablo Near Parras
Watercolor painted over words on the upper right, 4⁷/₁₆ x 3³/₄ inches

Chamberlain described Paso del Diablo as "a wild fearful looking place." It was, he wrote, "evidently of volcanic origin." He was surprised that no Mexican troops defended the place, which got its name, according to legend, when a priest tricked the devil into mining gold for him there. This could be labelled "Puerto de San Francisco" on Lieutenant Hughes's map of Wool's march. This is undoubtedly only a sketch.

Devil's Pass.

40. Parras
Watercolor, 8 x 13⅜ inches

Note the ever-present guerrillas behind the trees to the left of the picture. Sam and the other soldiers feared the guerrillas throughout the war.

◀

39. Devil's Pass
Watercolor, gouache, 10 x 6⁵⁄₁₆ inches, writing on verso

This is a much more careful rendition of Paso del Diablo, showing Wool's army marching through it towards Parras in the distance. Sam could not resist two melodramatic touches: the guerrilla spy and the ominous perched buzzard. Courtesy Anne S. K. Brown Military Collection, Brown University.

41. PARRAS
Watercolor, 7 x 12⅞ inches

42. Sam Dueling in a Bedroom

Pencil and watercolor, 4⅛ x 8¹/₁₆ inches, writing on gray paper on verso

Dropping in on his two Parras paramours, Nina and Rosita, Sam interrupts a coitus with a guerrilla. They duel. Rosita tells her lover Antonio, "mi Amor, pungar el gringo, y que la cama," or "stick the foreigner and come to bed." Sam responded by giving Antonio "a point in a part that made him howl with agony and would cause him to loos [*sic*] the regards of the dos margaritas."

pile of rocks, as I reached the Ground I look-
-ed an mine, while its hissing was reduc-
every moment to feel its coil around me,
not stopping to see the effect of the shot,
met the Sergant with the Guard, who wer
On the Sergant asking what was it
by an great Snake, and had shot it
but at the foot of the stones lay the G
carfully, and then they all burst out a
to be 4 „Inguana" a large spice of th
lenght. and its head as big as 4 foot ba
ACCESSION No. 15878c,
Picture #59 – Mexico City, interior of Cathedral
9/

around, and saw its fiery eyes still
-bled, I cocked my Carbine, and expecting
I took aim between the eyes and fired.
I turned and run, for the Guard, I soon
arlarmed by the report of my Carbine.
matter I replied that I had been attacked
When we reached the Cross, all was still
ject of my dread, all approached it
Laughting, for my big Snake proved
Lizzard, this one was over two foot in
ll, with eyes as large as dollars, being its
ACCESSION No. 15878e
Picture #60
"Cathedral in Monterrey."

43. SAM'S NIGHT OF THE IGUANA

Watercolor on two pieces of blue stationery. 5⅟₁₆ x 7¾ inches. Interior of Cathedral of Monterrey on verso. Same as number 19.

Sam, having drained a bottle of aguardiente, fell to daydreaming on a pile of rocks. Let him tell it: "A sharp hiss aroused me to the present. I sprang to my feet and caught sight of two bloodshot eyes . . . I could discern the outline of a hideous head, a wide mouth all horrent with teeth! Believing it a huge serpent, I gave one bound and landed on the ground expecting to feel the monster's coil around me every moment. Though in great terror, I took aim between the fiery eyes and fired, then turned and run for my life." The monster turned out to be a two-foot-long iguana.

44. March from Parras to Saltillo
Watercolor, 3⁹⁄₁₆ x 6⁷⁄₈ inches

At the news of Santa Anna's approaching army, Wool's army, on December 17, set out to join that of Taylor at Saltillo, but veered southeast to Rancho Agua Nueva.

45. Saltillo from the North
Watercolor, 3³⁄₁₆ x 5⁷⁄₈ inches

46. Main Cathedral in Saltillo
Watercolor, pencil, 5¹¹⁄₁₆ x 6¹¹⁄₁₆ inches

This is a crude watercolor sketch, probably Sam's first view of the cathedral.

47. CAPTAINS ENGLISH AND STEEN RUSH TO THE AID OF THE "RACKENSACKERS"
Watercolor, pen and ink, 2 x 6 inches, writing on verso

The Arkansas volunteers, in great consternation, report the approach of a large army. Dragoon Captains Steen and English ride out in haste to see for themselves. The Mexican "army" turns out to be wild mustangs.

48. Lt. Abraham Buford Scouting Out a Report of the Enemy
Watercolor, 5½ x 7 inches

This scene could be anywhere, but since news of Santa Anna's army caused Wool and Taylor to converge on Saltillo, this is probably Sam's commander or even General Wool himself on the lookout for Santa Anna's forces.

49. THE "MUSTANG ARMY" IN THE DISTANCE
Watercolor and ink on vertically lined paper, 3½ x 5 inches

The dust cloud in the right center of the picture is made by the herd of mustangs that the Rackensackers mistook for Santa Anna's army. Clearly all the American forces were edgy.

50. San Hosea [Jose] de Lavacayurea [La Vaqueria]
Watercolor, 4 x 7⁵⁄₁₆ inches, ruled paper, yellow

Note date 1846 on oven just below horses on left side of picture. Chamberlain called this a "miserable collection of adoba [*sic*] huts." It was a cattle ranch.

51. Señorita Offering Chocolate and Corn Cakes to Sam at Vacayurea [Vaqueria]
Watercolor, 3⅝ x 4¹/₁₆ inches

Both this and the preceding picture portray Sam's "mythical" advance ride with Lieutenant Carleton to Taylor's headquarters at Monterrey—a ride which Sam made up to place himself at the Battle of Monterrey, which took place before he ever left San Antonio with Wool's army.

52. AGUA NUEVA
Watercolor, 3¼ x 7 inches

Because of the cathedral, there is some reason to think that this might be a last view of Parras or a view of Saltillo. Sam and his fellow soldiers spent Christmas at Agua Nueva, however, and Sam described it as a "ganada," or cattle farm (note cattle to the left of the picture). He also refers to a "cuppla," or chapel, which in his recollection has grown into a cathedral.

53. TROOPS ON ROAD TOWARD SALTILLO VIA RINCONADA PASS
Watercolor, carelessly done, damaged lower left corner, 2⅛ x 4⅞ inches

Fearing an imminent Mexican attack, Taylor orders General Butler's troops to rush north from Monterrey to Saltillo on December 19, 1846.

54. General Wool Arriving at General Worth's Headquarters
Watercolor and gouache, 5½ x 10½ inches, writing on verso

General Wool arrived from Agua Nueva at General Worth's headquarters in Saltillo in a pelting rain in December 1846. He was held up outside in the rain by a sentinel and an orderly. According to Sam, "After some ten minutes the orderly returned with this message, 'Gen. Worth compliments to Gen. Wool and wishes to know what you want. What I want! exclaimed our little general, what I want! do you hear that Mr. McDowell? Tell General Worth that I want quarters for myself, staff and escort.' Away went the orderly," here pictured by Sam as an officious little servant, "and soon returned and said 'Gen. Worth says you can stop here.'"

Sam catches the ironic tone of the whole incident, in which the commander of the army is held up in the rain by an orderly shining a lamp into the face of Wool's aide, McDowell.

Rackensackers

96

the Rampage.

55. RACKENSACKERS ON THE RAMPAGE
Watercolor and pencil, 7³⁄₄ x 13¹⁄₂ inches. A gray page suggests some relation to the My Confession *ms.*

On February 10, 1847, Col. Archibald Yell's Arkansas Volunteers massacred Mexican civilians in a cave in the hills behind Agua Nueva. According to Chamberlain, "The cave was full of volunteers, yelling like fiends, while on the rocky floor lay over twenty Mexicans, dead and dying in pools of blood, while women and children were clinging to the knees of the murderers and shrieking for mercy."

56. Dragoons Rescue Survivors of Cave Massacre
Watercolor, 7¼ x 12¾ inches

Waving their "Arkansas toothpicks," 109 Arkansas volunteers surrender to the First Dragoons. Note now the relative calm of the Mexicans in the cave, as well as a slightly different cast of characters.

57. Sam on Picket Duty at Paso de los Pinos
Watercolor, 6⅛ x 7⅜ inches

Sam: "The wild night had its effect on me . . . and a horrid undefined sense of danger and fear took possession of my mind and I suffered all the agony of a coward when danger is nigh. In the gloomy woods, the trees ground and rubbed together producing strange unearthly noises. . . ."

58. THE PHANTOM
Watercolor, 3³/₁₆ x 2⁷/₁₆ inches

This old man could be a version of an apparition that Sam and several of the dragoons see and chase, though his costume does not include the "knee breeches" mentioned by Sam, and differs from the picture of the creature in *My Confession.* It also could be a picture of "Happy Jack Decker of Company A" of the Arkansas Volunteers.

"What in the d—l have you there Jack? [Sam's nickname was Peloncillo Jack] cried out the sergeant. 'The Old Boy himself, I believe,' I replied as I gave it another shot, when Gorman exclaimed. 'hold all, it is an old friend Tim McCarty from the old country' and tried to ride up to it. Holding out his hand he said 'Tim my boy, how are ye, how came ye out here, and what the d—l do you mean by twisting about in that ridiculous manner for? But Tim or whatever it was made no reply but kept its vortical [as in whirlwind] and erratic way. Gorman caught a look from the thing's fearful eyes, turned pale, and yelled out, 'a ghost! a ghost!' and went off on a run followed by all but four." Later, Sergeant Gorman "insisted that it was the ghost of Tim McCarty, come to warn him of his approaching death."

Capture of Maj Borlan command, at Incarnation.

59. Capture of Maj. Borlan [Borland's] Command, at Incarnation [Encarnación]
Watercolor and light gouache, 6¹⁄₁₆ x 7¼ inches, writing on verso describes the event

General Miñon, with a brigade of troops, surprises Major Gaines's command. Majors Gaines and Borland decided to surrender their command, consisting of Arkansas and Kentucky volunteers, on January 22, 1847.

60. RANGER DAN HENRIE ESCAPES FROM MEXICAN LANCERS
Watercolor and pencil, 6⁹⁄₁₆ x 12½ inches

When Major Gaines's command was captured by General Miñon's forces, he gave up his horse and pistols to daredevil Ranger Dan Henrie, who surprised the Mexican lancers and rode away, quickly outdistancing them on Gaines's Kentucky thorough-bred.

Escape of Dan. Henrie.

61. ESCAPE OF DAN HENRIE
Pen and ink, watercolor, 6³/₁₆ x 7 inches, writing on verso

This appears to be a later, more finished version of Dan Henrie's escape. It is from another angle and the scale, coloring, and detail are much different, as well as the direction of the riders. Both pictures show Henrie firing one of Major Gaines's two horse pistols, in the first scene with more success. Courtesy Anne S. K. Brown Military Collection, Brown University.

Ranche Hidiande.

62. RECONNAISSANCE AT RANCHO HIDIONDO [HEDIONDA]
Watercolor and gouache, 4¼ x 7 inches, writing on verso

Alarmed by reports of the approach of Santa Anna, on February 20, 1847, a reconnaissance in force led by Lieutenant Sturgis has a difficult ride up to the rancho, where they find Santa Anna's advance guard. Courtesy Anne S. K. Brown Military Collection, Brown University.

63. "Peloncillo Jack's" Sergeant takes a Tumble
Watercolor sketch, 2⁹⁄₁₆ x 3⁷⁄₈ inches

Disdaining Sam's advice, his sergeant leads his men through a prairie dog village in an attack on a ranch. According to Sam, when his horse's foot plunged into a hole, the sergeant was thrown headfirst into another hole. A large owl, followed by a "monstrous" rattlesnake, crawled out of the burrow. The sergeant exclaimed, "Holy Mother! Its the devil Peloncillo Jack, and no dog at all."

64. GENERAL WOOL AND HIS ENTOURAGE SCOUT OUT MONTERREY
Watercolor, 4³⁄₈ x 8¹⁄₈ inches

65. CAMP AT AGUA NUEVA
Watercolor and pencil, 4¹⁄₁₆ x 6¾ inches

Note the alarm of the Volunteers at Agua Nueva at the approach of Santa Anna's
army.

66. Camp at Agua Nueva
Watercolor, 4⅞ x 7 inches

A much more sedate view. Note supply train wagons, lower right, indicating that the regiment is ready to move to safety.

waiting for a Charge.

67. Burning of Our Camp at Agua Nueva ["Waiting for a Charge" on original]
Watercolor, 4½ x 6¼ inches

Under the command of, as Sam put it ironically, "Heroic Charley May . . . the Murat of America," General Taylor sent a reconnaissance in force to Hedionda, a ranch due east of Agua Nueva that stood astride a pass that would flank the American army. It was in fact on the very route General Miñon's cavalry was taking on its way to do just that. From the top of the ranch building, Sam spotted Mexican lancers. The American force hastily turned back toward Buena Vista, but not before burning the ranch and all its supplies. But see Karl Jack Bauer, *The Mexican War, 1846–1848*, p. 209, where he places the command under Col. Archibald Yell of Arkansas.

THE BATTLE OF BUENA VISTA

February 22–23, 1847

Plates 68–94

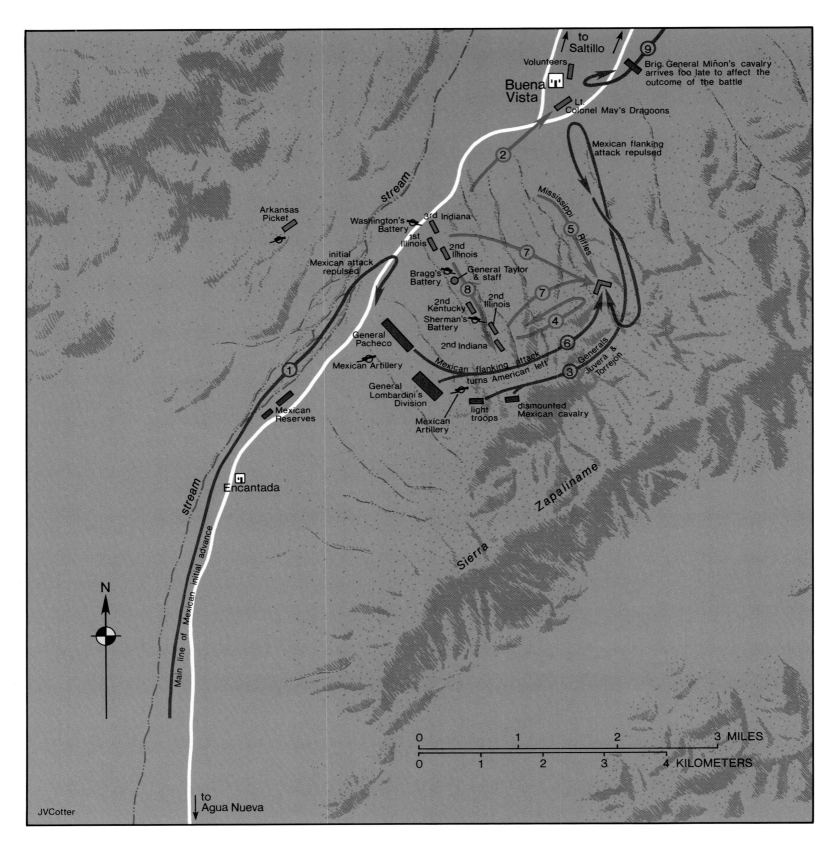

Arkansas
Picket

Washington's
Battery

3rd Indiana

1st
Illinois

2nd
Illinois

Bragg's
Battery

General Taylor
& staff

initial
Mexican attack
repulsed

2nd
Kentucky

2nd
Illinois

Sherman's
Battery

2nd Indiana

General
Pacheco

Mexican Artillery

Mexican Reserves

General
Lombardini's
Division

Mexican
Artillery

light
troops

dismounted
Mexican cavalry

Mexican flanking attack
turns American left

Generals
Juvera &
Torrejon

Encantada

to
Agua Nueva

Main line of Mexican initial advance

stream

stream

to
Saltillo

Buena
Vista

Volunteers

Brig. General Miñon's cavalry
arrives too late to affect the
outcome of the battle

Lt.
Colonel May's Dragoons

Mexican flanking
attack repulsed

Mississippi Rifles

Sierra Zapaliname

N

JVCotter

0   1   2   3 MILES

0   1   2   3   4 KILOMETERS

THE BATTLE OF BUENA VISTA

68. Fearing Encirclement at Hidiondo [Hedionda], Dragoons Hurry Back to Camp Buena Vista

Watercolor, 3⁵/₁₆ x 6⁷/₈ inches

Correctly fearing that Santa Anna might seize his supplies at Saltillo and Buena Vista, on the night of February 22 Taylor sent Archibald Yell's Arkansas Volunteers and 400 men of the Second Dragoons under Lt. Col. Charles May first to Hidiondo (Hedionda) and then to Saltillo, where they held off the Mexican flanking attack. Note flares fired by Miñon's forces.

Our Flight.

69. OUR FLIGHT FROM HIDIONDO [HEDIONDA] ["OUR FLIGHT" ON ORIGINAL]
Watercolor, gouache, 4 x 7 inches, writing on verso

This is another version of the dragoons hurrying back from Hidiondo to Buena Vista under Lieutenant Sturgis. Courtesy Anne S. K. Brown Military Collection, Brown University.

70. MEXICAN ARMY AT BUENA VISTA
Watercolor 6⁹/₁₆ x 12⁵/₁₆ inches

This is a view of the battlefield of Buena Vista from the Mexican point of view looking north. The Mexican army, emerging from La Angostura, looks out on the broad plain. From this view, they cannot see the deep gullies between them and the American troops in the distance. Mexican troops, however, are already starting down the "angostura," or deep wash, on the left, headed towards the burning Rancho Buena Vista. They will be met by Captain Washington's artillery battery and turned back.

71. SAM'S IMAGINED VIEW OF SANTA ANNA AND HIS GENERALS
Watercolor and pencil on yellow lined paper, 3 x 6¼ inches

The "Napoleon of the West" in a Napoleon hat and his chief officers, who are probably Gen. M. M. Lombardini (despite the fact that he led mostly infantry) or Cavalry Commander Gen. Julian Juvera (who led the charge on Buena Vista as well as on Jefferson Davis's Mississippi Rifles) in the red cavalry uniform; Pedro de Ampudia; Francisco Mejia; and Francisco Pacheco. Lombardini, who is to lead the major charge on the American left flank, seems to be pledging victory to his chief.

72. Grand Mass before Buena Vista
Watercolor and pencil, 3¼ x 6⁹⁄₁₆ inches. Note that picture is not quite finished.

"The sun rose bright and clear from behind the 'Sierra Frea' on the morning of the 23rd of February, 1847. . . . I doubt if the 'Sun of Austerlitz' [scene of one of Napoleon's great victories] shone on a more brilliant spectacle than the one before us. . . . Twenty thousand men clad in new uniforms, belts as white as snow, brasses and arms burnished until they glittered in the sunbeams like gold and silver . . . . Soon a procession of ecclesiastical dignitaries with all the gorgeous paraphernalia of the Catholic Church advanced along the lines, proceeded by the bands playing a solemn anthem. . . ." Sam exaggerated the number of troops; by this time there were approximately 15,000.

73. GENERAL WOOL ENCOUNTERS A BURSTING SHELL
Watercolor, pencil and gouache, 4⅞ x 6³/₁₆ inches, disciplined writing on verso

74. First Dragoons, Buena Vista, Night of February 22, 1847
Watercolor, some gouache, 6¼ x 11⁷⁄₁₆ inches

The First Dragoons, stationed as a mobile reserve behind the front lines, watch the Mexican flanking attack along the mountains to their left. Note officers pointing in that direction. Chamberlain reports, "Our Squadron dismounted and took the bits out of our horses' mouths and let them graze on the scarce dry grammer [*sic*] grass while we, seated at our ease on the ground viewed the drama being enacted on the mountain."

75. MEXICAN ATTACK ON LEFT AND CENTER OF AMERICAN LINES, NIGHT, FEBRUARY 22, 1847
Watercolor, gouache, 6¼ x 12⁵⁄₁₆ inches

This, in effect, was the opening of the battle in which Santa Anna would concentrate on turning the Americans' left flank while at the same time sending Lombardini's and Pacheco's cavalry regiments diagonally to the center left.

76. BATTLE AT THE PLAINS OF BUENA VISTA, FEBRUARY 23, 1847
Watercolor and gouache, 10 x 14¹/₁₆ inches

This is a strange panorama because General Taylor appears to be facing the wrong way, as is the entire army. In fact, he is ordering the dragoons in the gulley that he is facing to make haste to the front and center of the line. Far in the distance, one can see the red-shirted Mississippi Rifles in their famous V formation. Everything is backwards, as if in a mirror image. This differs from other panoramas of the battle by Chamberlain. See image in Harper's edition of *My Confession* and the obvious preliminary sketch for it in picture no. 75.

77. ANOTHER PANORAMIC VIEW OF THE BATTLE OF BUENA VISTA
Pen and ink, watercolor on yellow paper, 7¼ x 12¼ inches

This is an entirely different picture in scale, style, and content from Sam's puzzling mirror image view. It resembles his portrayal of the battle in *My Confession* (both the manuscript and Butterfield's Harper's edition of 1956). Yet this picture has more detail: many more wounded and dead, cannons, wagons, and Jefferson Davis's First Mississippi Rifles in the V formation. Being in an unfinished condition, however, this striking painting resembles a picto-map of the battle, with far more complexity than any other version. Courtesy Anne S. K. Brown Military Collection, Brown University.

78. GENERAL TAYLOR AND HIS STAFF, BUENA VISTA
Pencil drawing, no background, 10 x 14$^{1}/_{16}$ inches

Note Chamberlain, second from left in the back row of Taylor's guard. This is a beautifully composed little scene, with the wounded man looking straight at the viewer while a dead soldier sprawls before him, ignored by the general, who is intent on the intelligence he is receiving. General Taylor is normally described as wearing civilian clothes, but it is probable that in this battle he observed the rules of war and donned his uniform so that he might be identified by his own troops.

Rough and Ready
A little more grape Cap Bragg!

79. ROUGH AND READY: "A LITTLE MORE GRAPE CAP. BRAGG"
Watercolor and pencil, 3¹⁵/₁₆ x 3⁷/₁₆ inches

With cannonball whistling overhead, Chamberlain portrays Taylor casually telling Captain Bragg to load his guns with "a little more grape," which he probably did not say (see fn. 32, Introduction), but it has become part of the legend of the great battle and of Old Zach—a legend that helped carry him to the White House. Actually, it was a critical moment in the battle, because Captain O'Brien had just lost most of his guns and the Mexican attackers threatened to break the American line.

Capture of a Section of Washington Battery

80. CAPTURE OF A SECTION OF WASHINGTON'S BATTERY
Watercolor and pencil, 5¹⁄₁₆ x 8 inches

Chamberlain is confusing here. Though it *was* a section of Capt. John M. Washington's battery that was captured, it was that of the brave, beleaguered Capt. John Paul Jones O'Brien, whose three guns were part of Washington's battery. O'Brien's staunch holding of his position until virtually the last of his gunners was killed thwarted Lombardini's charge and played a major part in the American victory.

In this picture Chamberlain imagines that the battery was overwhelmed with benefit of clergy. For a more down-to-earth view, see plate 81.

The Capture of O'Brian Guns

81. THE CAPTURE OF O'BRIEN'S GUNS
Watercolor and pencil, 6⁷⁄₁₆ x 13¹⁄₁₆ inches

Capt. John Paul Jones O'Brien's artillery and the Second Indiana Regiment bore the full brunt of the main attack by 7,000 Mexican lancers and infantry. The Indiana regiment broke, but O'Brien bravely stood his ground until most of his artillerymen were killed or wounded. He then managed to retreat, losing all three of his guns.

82. THE HEROIC CHARLIE MAY: "COL. MAY YOUR SQUADRON IS *thar.*"
Watercolor, 4⅛ x 3⁵⁄₁₆ inches

Sam is caricaturing Lt. Col. Charles May. Like most soldiers, Sam never forgave May for taking credit for the capture of General De La Vega at the Battle of Resaca de la Palma, when the actual captor was a bugler, Private Winchell (Bauer, p. 65, fn. 27). Chamberlain implies that May was headed away from the battle when, at 9:00 A.M., Taylor appeared on the field with May's Second Dragoons and Jefferson Davis's Mississippi Rifles to save the day on the left flank.

83. MAJ. JOHN MUNROE TURNING THE 2ND INDIANA REGIMENT AROUND
Watercolor and pencil, 5¼ x 7⅛ inches

The Second Indiana had received the brunt of the Mexican attack under Gen. Julian Juvera on the mountainside that overlooked Taylor's left flank, and it had broken and fled, leaving the U.S. left flank almost entirely dependent on O'Brien's artillery, though the redoubtable Mississippi Rifles under Col. Jefferson Davis and the Third Indiana had just arrived on the field to save the day.

84. COMPANY, E, DRAGOONS, FIGHTING, BUENA VISTA
Watercolor and pencil, 6⅜ x 11¾ inches

Capt. D. H. Rucker's squadron of the First Dragoons save the supply train at Buena Vista from capture by a regiment of Mexican cavalry under Gen. Julian Juvera. Sam Chamberlain was with Rucker's squadron, which served under Lt. Col. Charles May.

Defeat of these Lancers by the Missippee Rifles

85. DEFEAT OF LANCERS BY THE MISSISSIPPI RIFLES ["DEFEAT OF THESE LANCERS BY THE MISSIPPEE RIFLES" ON ORIGINAL]

Watercolor and pen and ink, 5⅜ x 12⅛ inches

At 9:00 A.M. Taylor brought Davis's Mississippi Rifles onto the field from Saltillo. With the Third Indiana, the Mississippi Rifles formed a V, into which rode General Juvera's spirited horsemen, part of Maj. Gen. Francisco Pacheco's divison, where they were slaughtered. This seemed, for a time, to have turned the tide of battle, since it trapped a large part of Santa Anna's forces and demoralized his men. Note the excellent portrayal of the proud Mississippi Rifles, with their bright brass patch boxes on their 1841 rifles and their red jackets and white trousers. Also note that the general with the red tunic in the view of Santa Anna's generals is falling.

Gen Wool.
Leading the Illinois Reg to the Charge

86. GENERAL WOOL LEADING THE ILLINOIS REGIMENT TO THE CHARGE
Watercolor, 4⅛ x 3¹³⁄₁₆ inches

General Wool assumed immediate field command and rallied the Second Illinois, who charged back into the battle while the First Illinois surged forward, driving the enemy back and capturing the Hidalgo Battalion's flag, at the cost of losing their commander, Col. John J. Hardin.

87. BATTLE OF BUENA VISTA
Watercolor, gouache, 3⁹⁄₁₆ x 6¹¹⁄₁₆ inches

The U.S. troops are above, the Mexican troops below. La Angostura, to Taylor's right, is on the left here. Santa Anna's army is on the right of the picture.

88. In the Heat of the Battle at Buena Vista
Watercolor and gouache, 3⅞ x 6⅞ inches

This probably depicts the premature charge on the center of the Mexican lines by the Illinois and Kentucky regiments in which Henry Clay, Jr., was killed.

89. On the Battlefield the Night After the Battle
Watercolor and slight gouache, 3¹¹/₁₆ x 6¹³/₁₆ inches

Chamberlain remembered his picket duty on that night: "It was a cold night, with clouds scudding across the moon, which threw a weird light on the dismal scene. The ground strewn with ghastly corpses most of which had been stripted [*sic*] by our foes. A picket line of Mexican Lancers, mounted on white horses was stationed not over two hundred yards in my front."

90. SOLDIERS VISITING LT. COL. HENRY CLAY, JR.,'S GRAVE
Watercolor sketch, 2½ x 2⅜ inches

Lieutenant Colonel Clay, the son of Sen. Henry Clay, was killed while leading his Second Kentucky Regiment in an attack side by side with Colonel Hardin's Illinois Regiment at Buena Vista. For a daguerreotype view of Clay's temporary grave, see Martha A. Sandweiss, Rick Stewart, and Ben W. Huseman, *Eyewitness to War: Prints and Daguerreotypes of the Mexican War, 1846–1848* (Fort Worth: Amon Carter Museum; Washington, D.C.: Smithsonian Press, 1989), p. 119. Sam is a bit careless in this sketch.

91. COL. H. CLAY AND COL. J. J. HARDEN [HARDIN], BOTH KILLED AT BUENA VISTA
Watercolor and pencil, 4¹⁄₁₆ x 1¹³⁄₁₆ inches

The hacienda at Buena Vista appears in the background.

Capt. Enoch Stein

92. Cap. Enoch Stein [Steen]
Watercolor sketch, 3¹¹/₁₆ x 2¹/₁₆ inches, large handwritten note on verso

Capt. Enoch Steen was the company commander of Company E, First Dragoons. Though he consistently misspelled his name, Sam served with Steen, who had signed him up in San Antonio, for much of the northern Mexico campaign. It was Steen, not Stein, as Sam habitually misspelled his name, who broke Juvera's charge on the supply train at Buena Vista.

93. 1ST LEIU [*sic*] D. RUCKER
Watercolor sketch, 3⅝ x 1¹³⁄₁₆ inches, large handwriting on verso

Daniel Rucker of the First Dragoons was Sam Chamberlain's immediate superior officer. He lived to the age of ninety-five, the oldest living veteran of the Mexican War. He won a brevet to major for gallantry at Buena Vista. After the Mexican War he transferred to the Quartermaster Corps, and during the Civil War he was breveted to major general of volunteers in the Quartermaster Corps.

2nd Leiu. A. Beauford

94. 2ND LEIU [*sic*] A. BEAUFORD [*sic*]
Watercolor, pen and ink, 3¹³/₁₆ x 2 inches

First Lieutenant "Abe" Buford was also one of Chamberlain's officers in the Mexican campaign. He was a dashing, hell-for-leather cavalryman from Kentucky. Note his red hair. He became a Confederate general of cavalry under Nathan Bedford Forrest.

95. COL. YELL
Watercolor, pen and ink, 4 x 1⅞ inches

Col. Archibald Yell was the commander of the "Rackensackers," or Arkansas Volunteers. A hero in Arkansas but a relatively ineffective leader, he allowed his men to massacre civilians and at a crucial point in the defense of Buena Vista got into a seniority dispute with Col. Humphrey Marshall of Kentucky in the face of the oncoming Mexican cavalry. Most of the Arkansas Volunteers fled, except Yell himself, who was killed. Capt. Enoch Steen, with Sam Chamberlain and the Second Dragoons, saved the supply train at Buena Vista and hence the U.S. Army in Northern Mexico.

96. Camp Followers, Two Carrying Soldier on Litter
Watercolor Sketch, 4 x 7¼ inches

At Encantada, U.S. troops under Major Bliss and "Abe" Buford riding under a white flag come upon the Mexican wounded following the battle of Buena Vista. Sam wrote, "Death in its most terrible aspects lay around on every side, bodies torn and mutilated by bursting shells, ground into dust by ponderous cannon wheels, while the still more unfortunate, the wounded suffering a thousand deaths, from fearful wounds, hunger, thirst, cold, want of care, . . . and the uncertainty of their fate."

This picture shows some of the "hundreds" of women camp followers helping the wounded on burros and litters. Large details of U.S. soldiers with field ambulances also helped care for the Mexican wounded.

97. CAMP AGUA NUEVA, MARCH 1847
Watercolor and gouache, 6 x 12 inches

Lucifer leaps into Paradise.

98. LUCIFER LEAPS INTO PARADISE
Watercolor, pen and ink, 5½ x 8 inches, small handwriting on verso

Sam Chamberlain aboard his mighty Kentucky steed, Lucifer, leaping over an aloe hedge and adobe wall to rescue Don José Traveina's (Treveina's) wife and beautiful daughters, Tranceita [*sic*] and Delorious [*sic*], from two sex-crazed members of the Second Mississippi Rifles.

99. Sam and Tranceita watch sister "Lolo" dance with Sam's Sabre
Watercolor, gouache, pen and ink, 5³⁄₈ x 7¹⁄₄ inches

Sam wrote, "The two younger ladies were as lovely as the Peri of the Poet's dream." He fell in love with both of them, and vice versa. They urged him to select one, desert, and live happily ever after on their hacienda in Durango. Instead, a young Swede named Wallberg, a bugler in E Company, deserted and married Delorious [*sic*], and the entire family fled to Durango.

100. CHAMBERLAIN DOES IN THE BULLY OF COMPANY A
Watercolor and transparent gouache, 4⅞ x 8¾ inches

One dragoon, an Irish deserter from the British Army in Canada named Crane, had harassed Sam, stolen his drinking cup, and attacked him on several occasions. This scene represents one attack too many by Crane. Sam was cutting corn on the Treveina ranch with a broken sabre. With "Lolo" praying to the Virgin and Crane bellowing, "d—n you Peloncillo Jack, . . . I'll let out your heart's blood," our hero cooly sidestepped Crane's rushes, pinking him on the wrist, and finally, with no choice, "drove my blade to the hilt in his breast." Oddly, Sam drew himself with a moustache, which he never wore. Was this a disguise?

101. Mexican Guerrillas
Watercolor sketch, 6³/₈ x 10¹/

This took place near Alam
furious and decided to des
Juan Bautista Ranch.

On Guard.

102. ON GUARD
Watercolor sketch, 5⅞ x 8⅞ inches

Sam, with two Rangers, Tobin and Irvin, is at the door of Casa Blanca, the gateway to Buena Vista Ranch, to prevent other drunken Rangers under Ben McCulloch from savaging the ranch and its innocent inhabitants in retaliation for the deaths of the two men of the Quartermaster Corps.

103. THE BURNING OF ALAN
Watercolor sketch, 6⅝ x 10 iⁱ

Major Buford and the drag
taliation for the murder of ⁱ
its gate.

Rancho San Juan

104. RANCHO SAN JUAN BAUTISTA
Watercolor, 6½ x 7⅛ inches

105. "Carefree Life"
Watercolor, 5¾ x 7³/₁₆ inches, careful writing on verso

Sam duels dragoon Sgt. Tim Gorman over the Treveina girls. Gorman was eventually lassoed by the man coming through the doorway in the background. Later, with reinforcements, Gorman got even. He forced "his poluted [*sic*] lips" to "Delorioso" in spite of her resistance, and had Sam nearly clubbed to death.

ꜱADA TO THE LEFT ["RUINED

vertically lined yellow paper

Wool ordered Sam to ride
illo to Monterrey through
pt and a third returned to

ls something of his state of
scene contains a mammoth
erous crosses by the road–
rsty gang of 'salteadores.'"
full day's ride from Saltillo

107. "A Ride for Life"
Watercolor, 2⅞ x 12⅝ inches

A near duplicate of the previous picture, but more refined, with a slightly different angle and a picket guard on the horizon. The first of these was probably a sketch or study done on the back of a discarded version of *My Confession.* This suggests that perhaps Sam worked on two versions of *My Confession* at the same time.

108. HILL OF THE RINCONADA ["RINCONNADA" [*sic*] ON ORIGINAL]
Watercolor, 2⁹/₁₆ x 8⁷/₈ inches

Sam depicts the dramatic bare hills that line the dangerous route he had to take through the Barranca in order to complete the ride from Saltillo to Monterrey.

109. APPROACH TO "EL PASO DEL MUERTA [MUERTO]"
Watercolor, 2⁵/₈ x 3⁷/₈ inches, "Ruined ranch" written in top left corner

In his text Sam mentions approaching "El Paso del Muerta [*sic*]," "a wild dreary place, the road winding down the hill for nearly a mile and quite steep," with "numerous crosses on each side." Sam declares, "When nearly down I caught sight of a leather clad 'greaser,' watching me from the top of a small hill on the opposite side of the little stream that wound around the foot of the pass."

110. Camp Buena Vista ["(Outside Saltillo)" on original]
Watercolor, 3⁹⁄₁₆ x 13¹⁄₈ inches, on vertically lined paper, careful writing on verso

This shows Sam cantering along over what he believes to be a safe stretch from Buena Vista on the left to Saltillo in the center and Monterrey on the right. Note colorful cloud at right appears to be a torso portrait of a U.S. general, perhaps Taylor, in Sam's imagination. Also note how night turns into dawn, a favorite technique of Sam's to show a night's ride.

111. The Road to Monterrey
Watercolor, 2⁵⁄₈ x 13⁵⁄₈ inches

112. VALLEY OF THE SAN JUAN AT RINCONADA
Watercolor, 2³/₁₆ x 10½ inches

Though chased by fierce guerrillas (upper left) in this picture, Sam is more interested in showing the Valley of the San Juan and the dangerous pass.

113. THE BARRANCA
Watercolor, 4½ x 13¹⁵/₁₆ inches, careful writing on the back, gray paper

Here Sam is being chased down the steep trail of the Barranca by Romeo Falcon's bandits. The trail is so narrow and steep that Lucifer will not negotiate it. Sam ties a handkerchief over the horse's eyes and is able to lead Lucifer down the steep trail. The "barbarous foe" came at top speed on light ponies. Sam was, as he put it, "in a position of great peril." Note, however, that Sam seems to have made the bottom of the trail and shot one of his pursuers, who is falling to the bottom, with his long-range Hall rifle.

114. Hacienda de Buena Vista (Santa Caterina)
Watercolor, 3¾ x 7⅞ inches, careful writing on gray paper, verso

Just when Sam thought that he had outdistanced his pursuers and reached "the Hacienda de Buena Vista," really Santa Caterina, a few miles from Monterrey, he saw that more *salteadores* were there waiting for him.

115. ROAD TO MONTERREY, SHOWING CITY IN BACKGROUND AGAINST A BRILLIANT SUNRISE
Watercolor and pencil, 2 x 12⅛ inches

Interestingly, Sam travelled toward Monterrey from the west into the "brilliant sunrise." The scene actually depicts an all-night march from darkness at Santa Caterina rancho on the left, past Webster's battery in the right center, to Monterrey, with dawn breaking over it.

116. APPROACHING MONTERREY AT LAST
Watercolor and pencil, 2¼ x 12⅜ inches

Though one misses Saddle Mountain, which is behind the viewer, and other surrounding mountains in this picture, it does appear that Sam has reached La Purissima Bridge, Walnut Springs, and the Black Fort at Monterrey.

117. CHAMBERLAIN REPORTING WITH DISPATCHES TO GENERAL TAYLOR
Watercolor, 7³/₁₆ x 12⁵/₈ inches

While Sam salutes, General Taylor, in corduroy pants and vest, seems surprised that he made it through the guerrilla-infested country. Also present are Lt. Col. Charley May, Major Bliss, and a staff officer.

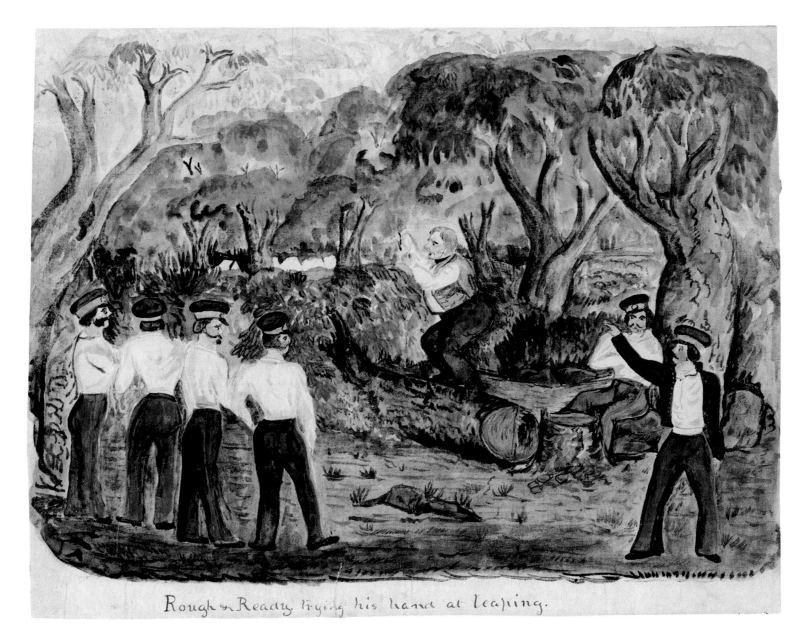

Rough & Ready trying his hand at leaping.

118. ROUGH & READY TRYING HIS HAND AT LEAPING
Watercolor, 6⅜ x 7⅞ inches, verso, illustrated heading to text on gray page "Dragoon Life in Camp and Field" on gray paper

The general at play while dragoons watch.

Capture of the Big Train
rors of War," Roman soldier
ipt of My Confession *and a*
it there might actually have
age in Introduction.

large government supply
d Fox' of Rio Grande ban-
oliad Texas." Sam got his
(Michael J.) Box, a wagon
long after Buena Vista, so

Massacre of the Big Train—escape of Capt. Box.

110 Wagons destroyed
130 Teamsters Killed

Near Ramas in Feb.ᵗʳʸ 1547

120. Massacre of the Big Train: Escape of Capt. Box
Watercolor and pencil, 7¼ x 13 inches

According to escapee Captain Box, he had "witnessed the most fiendish acts of wanton cruelty committed by the guerrillars [*sic*]. Teamsters was [*sic*] lassoed, stripted [*sic*] naked and then dragged through clumps of cactus and horribly mutilated, a boy of sixteen who drove a forge, was lashed in front of a bellows, a charcoale [*sic*] fire kindled and a fire hole blown into him until he expired in the most fearful agony. Another had a [*sic*] incision made in his abdomen, cartridges inserted and the victim blown up!"

In all, according to Chamberlain (and Box), 130 wagons were destroyed, 110 (actually 40–50) teamsters killed, and a "young Miss of sixteen was taken to Monte Morelos and made to sit as a nude centerpiece to the guerillar's banquet." (No one knows how Captain Box knew this or whether Chamberlain made this up.) See Bauer, p. 218.

Sam, however, was able to report with some satisfaction, "Three wagons loaded with ammunition blew up killing a number of the yelling devils."

121. Gen. Caleb Cushing
Watercolor and pen, 4¹¹/₁₆ x 3³/₈ inches

Caleb Cushing, a brigadier general from Massachusetts appointed by President Polk, "with a rare discretion, only exceeded by his disregard of all considerations," according to Sam, visits Saltillo. He had briefly commanded New England volunteers and the North Carolina, Virginia, and Second Mississippi Rifles, who arrived late in 1847 at Buena Vista, which perhaps accounts for Sam's malicious description of General Cushing. He is smitten by a señora, "one of the most ravishing beauties the world has seen since Helen of Troy." Cushing follows the train all the way until he "has his way" with the señora. Cushing had been the first U.S. commissioner to China, in 1843, which he opened up to U.S. trade in a treaty of 1844. Later, after the war, he twice ran unsuccessfully for governor of Massachusetts, was appointed to the Massachusetts Supreme Court, and later failed as nominee for the U.S. Supreme Court due to wicked partisan politics, as he was one of the country's most formidable legal scholars. The following vicious stanza by James Russell Lowell indicates what Massachusetts Whigs thought of Cushing after his 1841 switch from Whig to Democrat.

General C. is a dreffle smart man;
He's been on all sides that give places or pelf;
But consistency still waz a part of his plan—
He's been true to one party and that is himself.

As Cushing had a wife and children back home, this picture bears out Lowell's wicked verse.

Halt at "Molino del Rey"

122. HALT AT "MOLINO DEL REY"
Watercolor sketch, 4⅜ x 2¼ inches

This is confusing. It is not the site of the Battle of Molino del Rey outside Mexico City, but another *molino*, or mill site, where Sam and his comrades downed a little "muscal" and waited for the train bearing the amorous General Cushing and his señora to catch up after they had finished their dalliance, which took almost exactly two hours.

El Fandangoé.

123. FANDANGO AT MONTERREY ["EL FANDANGOE" ON ORIGINAL]
Watercolor and pencil, 5¹⁄₁₆ x 7³⁄₈ inches

Note that again Sam has a moustache.

124. Sam Sketching Valley of Zacatecas
Watercolor, gouache over graphite, 3¾ x 6⅜ inches

On the scout south to Zacatecas under Lieutenant Carleton the detachment went into camp at a well-watered ranch with a view. Carleton and Sam (Peloncillo Jack) climbed a high mesa rising from the plain. "Carleton dismounted and said, 'Jack bring up your sketch book, you will find a grand view from here.'" Sam is shown here sketching "a beautiful valley of bright green thickly studded with the white walls of Haciendos [*sic*] Ranches [*sic*] churches and convents, while away in the distance rose the towers and domes of a great city, the city of Zacatecas." Also note Carleton "using his field glass." From this point, they looked towards Mazapil and saw Santa Anna's retreating army, especially the glistening lances of Miñon's division.

125. MINIATURE OF A CITY
Watercolor, 1¼ x 6¹/₁₆ inches

This may be Zacatecas, which Sam sketched and described as "a great city" with "towers and domes."

Flogging a Alcalde

126. Flogging a [*sic*] Alcalde
Pen and ink, watercolor, gouache, 6⁹⁄₁₆ x 7½ inches, writing on verso

At a ranch on the road to Zacatecas, Major Buford's command stopped to have their horses shod, but the farrier's tools were mysteriously missing. Buford had the alcalde, or mayor, stripped to the waist and tied to a wagon wheel. Then he ordered him flogged—"give the old rascal a taste of the blacksnake, Sherrod"—until the tools were forthcoming. The figure behind the alcalde is Buford; Sherrod wields the whip; and on the distant peak Ranger scouts see the glistening lances of a large Mexican force. Courtesy Anne S. K. Brown Military Collection, Brown University.

127. "Caveat Actor"
Pen and ink, 3³⁄₁₆ x 7½ inches, writing on verso

Sam, first on the left, "bucked and gagged," watches one "John Dougherty" (this must be former private Austin Daugherty of Company F), lately discharged from the First Illinois Volunteers, being given fifty lashes at Maj. Thomas W. Sherman's orders for selling liquor to the troops. Sam had refused to do the flogging and hence he was punished by Sherman, under whom he was later to serve in the Civil War. Dougherty [*sic*] was cut to ribbons and Sherman wanted to leave him to die. The enlisted men put him on a burro and got him medical attention.

Bucking consisted of running a long pole under the knees while in a sitting, knees-up position, then tying the hands in front of the knees. Sam additionally was gagged with a large tent peg that nearly broke his jaw. Courtesy Anne S. K. Brown Military Collection, Brown University.

128. PESQUERIA GRANDE
Watercolor and ink, 4 x 7½ inches, writing on verso soaked through in the sky

"Pesqueria Grande," on the road to Monterrey, seen on mountain with cross on the left, means "Big Fishery," presumably from the lake or river in the foreground. In the center of the picture, traced on the hills by white lime rock, is a representation of Christ crucified.

129. Sam Shooting Mexican Pursuer
Watercolor and pencil, 3⅞ x 6¼ inches

Sam saves his enemy Lieutenant Wilson outside of Pesqueria Grande. Wilson, aroused by Sam from a dalliance with a señorita just as a band of guerrillas was approaching, let his horse get away from him. Sam dismounted and, with his carbine, "had the good fortune to knock one out of the saddle." The pursuers then held up, allowing Sam and Wilson to escape.

Monterey from the Bishop Palace, and Shooting of A Horse Theif

130. MONTERREY, BISHOP'S PALACE AND VIEW OF TOWN ["MONTEREY FROM THE BISHOP'S PALACE, AND SHOOTING OF A HORSE THEIF" [*sic*] ON ORIGINAL]
Watercolor and pencil, 7⁵/₁₆ x 12¹/₁₆ inches

Sam set out to sketch Monterrey from the Bishop's Palace when two men tried to knife him and steal his horse Lucifer. Sam confronted the knife-wielder with his pistol. "I shot at him but missed the rascal." Note that in this picture, which is less finished than the following scene, the coloring and the exterior of the Bishop's Palace are different. Sam must have made these pictures at different times and, in at least one of these two pictures, possibly from memory. Note that the palace, the view, and the city are somewhat different from the version that follows.

131. The Shooting of a Horse Thief
Watercolor and pencil, 7¼ x 12¾ inches

The other thief cut Lucifer's lariat loose and, riding like a Comanche on the side of the horse, dashed down the hill. Sam, as shown here, shot him; he died, and Sam reclaimed his horse.

132. SAM WITH PISTOL IN THE PROCESS OF RESCUING CARMELEITA FROM "EL TUERTO"
Watercolor sketch, 3⅞ x 7¾ inches, careful writing on gray paper, verso

Here the evil "El Tuerto," with whom Sam had fought at the San Nicholas house of prostitution, was about to beat his new peon wife for running away on their wedding day. But Sam is too chivalrous and just could not bring himself to shoot even "El Tuerto" in the back. Instead, he rushed up to him, pointed the gun at his good eye, and then foolishly let him run away; he would return. Meanwhile Sam "took her under his wing." Sam has a moustache here—another disguise?

133. Carmeleita Moves in with Sam
Watercolor, 5⅛ x 7¼ inches

Sam takes Carmeleita as his mistress and has some of the best days and nights of his life.

134. UNDER A TREE AT SAN NICHOLAS, SAM TOASTS CARMELEITA'S HEALTH
Watercolor and pencil, 4 x 3⅜ inches. Note large letter "R" and other writing to the right of the picture. This appears to be the start of a chapter. Writing on gray paper, verso.

Sam here seems to be using or reusing scrap paper. Did he do a number of revisions of pictures at the same time? Moustache mysteriously reappears.

La Belle Carmeleita.

39

135. La Belle Carmeleita
Watercolor and gouache, 7¾ x 7¾ inches, careful writing on gray paper. Verso appears to have been done after the picture and to have soaked through it.

Sam bought Carmeleita new clothes and a horse of her own, on which she gallops about happily.

136. Sam Chamberlain Searching for Carmeleita

Watercolor, dark, almost opaque, 3⅜ x 6⅝ inches, writing on verso, gray paper

"El Tuerto" reclaimed Carmeleita with the help of the U.S. authorities (the wife of another, she was living illegally in the military camp), then murdered her. Sam, not knowing where she had gone, searched day and night for her. He eventually learned from his friend "the Guerillar Priest" that "El Tuerto" took Carmeleita to Canales's hideout, where "she was outraged by the whole gang of demons and then cut to pieces."

▶

137. Burning of Haunted Mission San Ildefonso

Watercolor, opaque, 11⅛ x 6¹³⁄₁₆ inches

This abandoned mission populated by bats and owls seemed haunted to Sam and his cohorts. Manuel, their guide, called it a "casa del diablo" (devil's house). It was an Indian pueblo structure with a belfry that rang continuously for no reason at all. The dragoons set fire to it, but they could still hear the bells tolling from the "haunted" mission.

138. Taking a Salteador Stronghold

Watercolor, gouache and pencil, 8 x 7³⁄₁₆ inches, painted over page of notes

The Mexican guerrillas (*salteadores*) were holed up in a stone ranch house that seemed impregnable; as Sam put it, "It was certainly a hard nut to crack without artillery." But Sam noted a weakness: "the leaves of the gate opened inwardly." He reported this to Captain Buford, who dismounted his men and kept up a steady fire to distract the defenders. Then five brave men took up a plow and ran it into the gate as a battering

▶

139. THE LEGEND OF MONTE MORELOS AND THE COLUMN OF INDEPENDENCE
Watercolor, 5 x 7³/₁₆ inches

The eerie ruins of what was said to have been the most magnificent edifice in the New World, designed by a Tuloc, Torrescortez, otherwise known by his Christian name, "Imanuel." Betrayed by the bishop after building the majestic edifice, Torrescortez/Imanuel destroyed it as if by magic. The whole story of this legend is in Chamberlain's original manuscript, but was left out of Roger Butterfield's later printed version.

◄

ram. The guerrillas shot two of them and howled with delight as the other two ran for cover. But then Sam and three others ran forward, siezed the plow, and bashed in the gate. The dragoon unit, dubbed the "forlorn hope," charged with pistols and cold steel. Except for the pistols, it was a scene right out of a Walter Scott novel. Sam was sorely beset by a host of guerrillas; he held them off until help came, then nearly decapitated the renegade guide Antonio; or, as he put it, "I parried an ugly thrust and gave a clean stroke on his bare neck, the steel cut through bone and gristle to the center, and the renegade guide, with a curse on his lips, fell dead."

FROM A OLD PAINTING IN MONT MORELAS.

San Idelfonso.

140. Palace of San Idelfonso [*sic*] from a [*sic*] Old Painting in Monte Morelas [*sic*]
Watercolor, ink, gouache, 7⅝ x 13½ inches, careful writing on verso, gray paper

This is an intriguing picture of the great structure built by Torrescortez / Imanuel, which had a dome larger than St. Peter's, just before he destroyed it. To the left are the Tuloc Teocalli and the pagan priests, holding up their hands and cursing the perfidious bishop, who burned Imanuel's sister, mother, and promised bride at the stake, then planned to have the Inquisition burn all of the 900 Tuloc builders. The Dominican friar who told Sam this strange story is seen as a prisoner on the Teocalli at the foot of a ferocious-looking idol. Only he survived to tell the tale, which he did to Sam at the Column of Independence in Monte Morelos.

141. Night Errantry in Mexico
Watercolor and gouache, 4 x 7 inches

As Sam and the dragoons rode away from Monte Morelos, the haciendas they passed "appeard [*sic*] like stately castles." That night, bivouacked at Hacienda Las Chinipas, they chanced to see a blonde woman who had "large melancholy eyes and seemd [*sic*] to ask for protection!" Sam and his comrades believed she was an American prisoner. They saw a dark, evil-looking man dragging her away from a barred window and, says Sam, "we were convinced . . . that we had stumbled on a full blown romance, Old Castle, Lovely damsel in distress, Ruffian Jailor [*sic*], all as plain as a pikestaff."

That night Sam and his comrades broke through the wooden bars and Sam fought off the "Ruffian Jailor," a stage villain type, while the damsel in question clung to Sam's leg in fright, breasts exposed. Sam flipped the jailer's rapier out of his hand; the dragoons—note Buford with gun—pointed their pistols at the villain and rescued the damsel in distress. It was a romance novel tale.

142. THE EXECUTION OF VICTOR GALBRAITH
Watercolor, 3⅞ x 7¼ inches

Galbraith, a Prussian in the First Illinois Regiment, found his Mexican mistress in bed with Capt. Gaston Mears. Galbraith threatened to kill Captain Mears, but was captured, tried, found guilty of threatening a superior officer, and sentenced to death, a sentence approved by General Taylor himself. This scene shows Galbraith, blindfolded, kneeling next to his coffin and grave, singing Lutheran hymns, surrounded by troops and about to die by firing squad as the sun rises on December 28, 1847.

143. AN EXPERIMENTAL EXECUTION
Watercolor and pencil, 3⅜ x 7½ inches

In 1846 five volunteers serving under General Patterson at Camargo were sentenced to death for "insubordination." It was an experiment to throw fear into the hearts of all the other troops. Three men were secretly pardoned and fired at with blank cartridges. One fell dead without a scratch. Another became "a gibbering idiot," while the third expressed a wish that they would "stop their dogon fooling and that their shooting wasn't worth shucks."

144. THE SAN PATRICIO EXECUTION AT MIXCOAC
Watercolor, pencil, 6¹³⁄₁₆ x 12³⁄₁₆ inches

The execution of San Patricio deserters was done not only as Chapultepec fell but earlier at San Angel and Mixcoac, where fifty died in all on successive days. Chamberlain was not present at this event.

145. THE HORSE FORT FIGHT AT AGUA FRIO [*sic*]
Watercolor, ink, and gouache, 4⅛ x 6¼ inches

Near Ceralvo, a troop led by Lt. Reuben P. Campbell was attacked by a large body of guerrillas with a cannon mounted on a donkey (dubbed by the dragoons "The Jackass Artillery"). The Mexicans fired the cannon once and the jackass collapsed. Sam's horse Lucifer was killed. So were most of the other dragoons' horses, as they shot their own steeds and formed a barricade of horses. A German trooper, Necklin, rode for help and reinforcements arrived in time.

146. TUCSON, ARIZONA, 1848
Watercolor and pencil sketch, 3¼ x 5⅞ inches

Chamberlain claims to have painted this while handcuffed by order of drunken Maj.
L. P. Graham, who objected to his sketching. He did several other more-finished pictures of Tucson that cast doubt on the accuracy of this one.

147. PROBABLY TUCSON

Watercolor, pencil, 3 x 3¹¹/₁₆ inches, loose writing on gray paper, verso. Not typical of usual handwriting.

This was also probably done while Sam was handcuffed. He did, however, execute some carefully drawn pictures of Tucson that appear in *My Confession*. They are much different from these pictures.

148. Road to Mexico City
Watercolor, 2¹/₁₆ x 6¹¹/₁₆ inches, writing on gray paper, verso

On March 9, 1848, Gen. Winfield Scott launched an amphibious attack against Vera Cruz, Mexico. By 11:00 P.M., 8,600 U.S. troops had landed on the beaches around Vera Cruz with no casualties. This force included General Worth's division of 5,000 men and major units under colonels Patterson and Twiggs. Many of these troops, drawn from General Taylor's Army of the North, had marched to Brazos Santiago and boarded ships for Vera Cruz. Sam Chamberlain was not among these forces. Therefore his paintings of this campaign were either pure imagination or, as is more likely, drawn from other pictorial sources. For the most part, they are inaccurate.

Consequently, this plate and plate 149 are set off from Sam's other Mexican War pictures.

The existence of these few pictures seems to indicate that Chamberlain had some idea of producing an illustrated history of the whole war, but soon gave it up.

149. Execution of Legion San Patricio Before Chapultepec
Watercolor, gouache, pencil, 3¾ x 7³⁄₁₆ inches

Members of the San Patricio Battalion (of American deserters to Mexico) were seated backwards in wagons with ropes around their necks and, at the raising of the American flag over Chapultepec, the wagons were pulled out from under them. It was a mass execution.

150. PEACE
Watercolor, pencil and gouache, 1¾ x 7⁷⁄₁₆ inches, writing on gray paper on verso

The symbolism of this picture is obvious but revealing. Peace reaches from Masonic Washington and its classical capitol across the Rio Grande to the cathedral and cross representing Catholic Mexico, with its mountains and plains. It is the dawn of a new age, thinks Sam, who remains obdurately anti-Catholic. Some believe the Mexican War never ended.

INDEX

(pictures are indicated by **bold faced** page numbers)

Abilene Christian College: ix

Abolitionists: 7

Adams, Charles Francis, II: 15, 33n.50

Admirable Crichton, The (play): 31n.2

Africa: Chamberlain in, 15

Agua Nueva. *See* Rancho Agua Nueva

Ainsworth, William H.: x, 28; his influence on Sam, 31n.3

Alamo Ranch: guerrillas near, 149; burning of, **151**

Alcazar, the (Seville): 61

Aldie Courthouse: 16

Alton, Illinois: **40**

Alton (Illinois) Guards: Sam joins, 11; mutiny of, **41**

American Star, The: war accounts in, ment., 7

Amon Carter Museum: ix

Ampudia, Pedro de: **116**; map adapted from, **4**

Anderson, Joseph: 14

Anderson, Nancy: ix

Annapolis, Maryland: Sam at camp at, 16

Antonio: Sam duels with, **27**, 28, **84**

Apache Indians: army supply lines vulnerable to, 5; J. Glanton hunts, 14

Appomattox: surrender at, ment., 16

Arizona: Sam in, ment., x, 14, 26; U.S. gains from Mexican War, 3. *See also* Tucson, Arizona

Arizona Historical Society Library: x

"Arkansas toothpick." *See* bowie knife

Arkansas volunteers ("Rackensackers"): 25, **88**, **96–97**, **98**; J. Decker of, 100; surrender of, **101**

Army of the Potomac: at Cold Harbor, 16; Sam with, 21

Artists and Illustrators of the Old West: xi

Austin Colony: M. Gray of, **8**

Australia: gold seekers from, 3

Averell, Gen. W. W.: Sam with, 16, 21

Aztecs: 25; Sam's tales of, ment., 28

Baird, David: x

Baja California: Sam in, ment., x; attempted takeover of, 15

Bandera Pass: J. Hays fights Comanches at, 8

Barranca, the: Sam approaches, **156**, **158**

Barre, Massachusetts: Sam retires in, 15, 19

Barrie, J. M.: 31n.2

Baton Rouge, Louisiana: young Sam finds work at, 11

Battle of Buena Vista: **115–136**; Sam's description of, now missing, xi, 60; Taylor's victory at, ment., 7; Sam in, 12, 14, 28; map of, **112**; attack on supply train during, 131, 139, 142, **163–164**, **165**; the night after, **136**; camp followers and wounded at, **143**; C. Cushing at, 166

Battle of Cerro Gordo: W. Scott at, ment., 7

Battle of Culpepper Courthouse: Sam in, 16

Battle of Manassas: Sam and, 15–16

Battle of Molino del Rey: 25, 167

Battle of Monterrey: **53–63**; J. Hays at, ment., 8; Sam's source for, 8; Sam and, 12, 20, 25, 32n.31, 53, 63, 64, 67, 92; map of, **52**; Wool's army and, 67, 71

Battle of Resaca de la Palma: C. May at, 128

Battle of St. Mary's Church: 15; Sam in, 16

Battle of San Jacinto: monument at site of, 1; M. Gray in, 8

Battle of San Pascual: S. Kearny at, 5–6

Bauer, Karl Jack: 109, 165

Baylee, Capt. *See* Baylor, Capt. Henry W.

Baylor, Capt. Henry W.: **8**

Beale, Lt. Edward Fitzgerald: 32n.6

Bexar County: 11

Bexar Exchange saloon (San Antonio): **44–45**; fights at, 1, 11

Bibles: Chamberlain's collection of, 19

Billy Budd (novel): 31n.2

Bishop's Palace (Monterrey): Texas Rangers at, 12, **18**, 25, 32n.25, **56–57**, **58**; storming of, 55; Sam claims to be wounded at, 64; Monterrey viewed from, **175**

Bissell, William H.: 11

Black Fort, the (Monterrey): surrender of, **61**; Sam arrives at, **161**

Bliss, Maj.: **143**, **162**

Borland, Maj.: capture of, **101**

Boston, Massachusetts: Sam grows up in, 10, 26

Boston *Globe*: war accounts in, ment., 7

Bowditche family: 15

bowie knife: Sam sees man killed with, 1; Sam acquires, 11; Arkansas volunteers use, **98**

Box, Michael J. ("Mick"): and attack on supply train, 164, **165**

Bracito (El Paso): battle at, ment., 7

Bragg, Capt.: Taylor's instructions to, 12, 32n.32, **125**

Bravo, The (novel): 28

Brazos Santiago: Taylor's troops ship to Vera Cruz from, 195

Britain: effect of Mexican War on, 3

Brown, Chamberlain: 23, 31n.2

Brown, George: 23. *See also* Chamberlain, Delorious Trevino

Brown, Lyman: 23, 31n.2, 34n.69

Brown Military History Collection. *See* Brown University

Brown University, Anne S. K. Brown Military History Collection: paintings in, ment., ix, 21, 23, 25, 31n.3; Chamberlain works courtesy of, **13, 18, 27, 46, 59, 64, 69, 70, 77, 80, 103, 104, 114, 123, 171, 172**

Buena Vista: scholars inspect battle site at, ix; Americans retreat from Agua Nueva toward, 109, **114**; Dragoons hurry back to, **113**; hacienda at, **138, 159**; attempted savaging of ranch, **150**; camp at, **157**. *See also* Battle of Buena Vista

buffalo soldiers: Chamberlain commands, 16, 19

Buford, Lt. Abraham: **89, 141, 143,** 184, **187**; and burning of Alamo Ranch, 151; has alcalde whipped, **171**

Bullock: Gov. (Mass.): 19

Butler, Gen.: Taylor orders to Saltillo, 94

Butterfield, Roger: editing of *My Confession* by, xi, 1, 26, 31n.1, 34n.69, 123, 185; on Chamberlain, 15

Cabot, Louis: 15

California: U.S. gains from Mexican War, 3; Sam leaves with expedition for, 14. *See also* Baja California

Camargo, Mexico: execution at, **189**

Cambridge, Massachusetts: Chamberlains settle in, 15

Campbell, Lt. Reuben P.: 192

Camp Parole (Annapolis, Md.): Sam at, 16

Canales, Antonio: renegade bandits of, 19; Sam writes about, 28; attacks supply train, 164; Carmeleita taken to hideout of, 182

Captain May's Quickstep (music): 35n.77

carbine. See *escopeta*

Carleton, Lt. James H.: Sam accompanies, 12, 64, 92, 169

Carr, William: 14

Carson, Kit: rescues S. Kearny, 5

Casa Blanca (gateway to Buena Vista Ranch): guerrilla fighting near, **149, 150**

Castle of Ulloa (Vera Cruz): 7

Castroville, Texas: Ritter's farm in, 11; Sam at, **46**

Catholics: in Aztec Mexico, 25; Sam remains anti-, 197

Centre Harbor, New Hampshire: Sam born in, 10

Ceralvo, Mexico: Horse Fort fight near, **192**

Chamberlain, Carmeleita Hampton: 15

Chamberlain, Delorious Trevino: 15, 23

Chamberlain, Mary Keith: Sam marries, 15; china collection of, 19; and ms of *My Confession*, 23

Chamberlain, Samuel Emery: as prison warden, x, 19; painting albums of, provenance, xi, 23; his bigotry toward Mexicans, xii; and guerrillas, 6, 154, 156, **158, 184, 192**; birth and background of, 10; romantic character of, 10, 19, 28, 29, 31n.2, 187; runs away from home, 10–11; acquires bowie knife, 11; jailed in San Antonio, 11; joins Wool's army, 10, 11; with Alton Guards, 11, **41**; at Buena Vista battle, 12, 25, 28; and Monterrey battle, 12, 20, 25, 32n.31, 53, 63, 64, 67, 92; horses of, 12, **146, 154, 155, 158,** 175, 177, 192; maiden charge of, **13**; paints Grand Canyon, 14; in California, 14–15; rescues Carmeleita, 14, **24,** 28, **178, 179, 180, 181, 182**; with filibusterer Walker, 15; marriage and family of, 15; world cruise of, 15; Civil War career of, 15–16, 19; weapons collection of, 15, 19; accepts command of buffalo soldiers, 16, 19; Civil War wounds of, 16, 19–20, 21, 26; appointed assistant quartermaster general, 19; attends veterans functions, 19; Bible collection of, 19; death and burial of, 20; photographs of, 20–21, 23, **30**; eightieth birthday of, 26; duels with Antonio, **27**, 28, **84**; and Traveina sisters, 28, **146**, **147**, **153**; odd lots of paintings by, uncovered, 31n.3, 34n.72; Mexican War service record of, 32n.31; literary influences on, 35n.77; at Castroville, **46**; sketchbook of, 49, 63; enters Monclova, **69**; paintings from delirium, **70**, **84**; at Vaqueria, **92**; on duty at Paso de los Pinos, **99**; nickname of, 100; in Taylor's guard, **124**; does in bully, **148**; rides through guerrilla country, **154–162**; at Monterrey fandango, **168**; "bucked and gagged," **172**; shoots horse thief, **176–177**; and Vera Cruz attack, 195; anti-Catholic, 197. See also *My Confession*

Chamberlain, Tranceita Maria: 15, 23

Chapultepec, Mexico: heroes from, ment., 3; capture of, 25, 191, 196

Charlestown, Massachusetts: Sam and prison at, x

Chihuahua, Mexico: capture of, 7

Civil War, the: Sam in, 15–16, 19–20, 21; buffalo soldiers in, 16, 19

Claflin, Gov. (Mass.): 19

Clarksville, Texas: Sam's buffalo soldiers sent to, 16, 19

Clay, Col. Henry, Jr.: **138**; killed, 135; grave of, **137**

cloud portrait: **157**

Col. Cross (steamer): **48**

Col. Taylor (steamer): **48**

Cold Harbor: Sam at, 16

Colorado: U.S. gains from Mexican War, 3

Comanche Indians: army supply lines vulnerable to, 5; Wool passes through country of, 7, **67**; J. Hays fights, 8; chiefs under Santana, **9**; Sam's paintings of, ment., 12

Confederate cavalry: 16

Connecticut State Library (Hartford): x

Connecticut State Prison (Wethersfield): Sam warden of, x, 19, 26

Conquest of Mexico, The: 25, 35n.77

Cooper, James Fenimore: 28

Cotter, John V.: x

Couts, Cave J.: 14

"cowboys, the": M. Gray's raiders called, 8

Craighead, A. M.: 34n.72

Crain, John: ix–x

Crichton (romance novel): 31n.2

Crowinshield family: 15

Currier, Nathaniel: 35n.77

Cushing, Gen. Caleb: **166**, 167

Custer, Gen. George: Sam with, 16

Daily Alta California: x

Dameral, Mrs. George S.: ix, 23, 31n.3, 34n.72, 164

Davis, Jefferson. *See* Mississippi Rifles

Decker, Jack: possible picture of, **100**

de la Vega, Gen.: capture of, ment., 128

dervishes and devils: Sam's tales of, ment., 28

Dinwiddie Court House: 16

Doniphan, Alexander: volunteer army of, 5; crosses desert to capture Chihuahua, 7

doughboys: first use of term, 11, 32n.25

Dougherty, John [Austin]: receives lashes, **172**

East Indies: Sam in, 15

Education of Henry Adams, The: 31n.2

Eisenhower, John: ix; on Sam's romantic nature, 10; on Chamberlain paintings, 12

El Paso. *See* Bracito (El Paso)

El Paso del Muerto: **156**

El Tuerto: Sam's portrayal of, 14, **24**, 28, **178**; murders Carmeleita, 182

Encarnación, Mexico: Borland captured at, **101**

Enchanted Rock: J. Hays fights Comanches at, 8

English, Capt.: **88**

escopeta: **75**, **76**

Eyewitness to War: Prints and Daguerreotypes of the Mexican War, 1846–1848: 137

Falcon, Romeo: 154, 158

fandango: 28, **64**, **168**

Fanny (Boston danseuse): 10

Far East: effect of Mexican War on, 3

Fayette County: company of Rangers from, ment., 8

Fifth Massachusetts Cavalry: Sam commands, 16

First Dragoons: Sam joins, 11; Arkansas volunteers surrender to, **98**; at Buena Vista battle, **119**, 139

First Illinois Volunteers: at Buena Vista battle, **133**; J. [A.] Dougherty of, **172**; V. Galbraith of, **188**

First Massachusetts Cavalry: Sam with, 15, 16, 33n.50

Florida. *See* Seminole War (Florida)

Ford, Gov. (Ill.): 41

Ford, John Salmon "Rip": at Palmito Ranch, 16

Forrest, Nathan Bedford: 141

Fort Brown: **48**; federals flee to, 16

Foster, Stephen: 35n.77

France: and invasion at Vera Cruz, 7; and raid on Rio Grande, 19; Spanish war with, 74

Frank Leslie's Illustrated Weekly: clippings from, illustrate album, 21

Fredericksburg, Texas: fight with Comanches near, 8

Frost, John: 35n.77

Furber, George C.: 35n.77

Gaines, Maj.: surrender of, 101, 102, 103

Galbraith, Victor: execution of, **188**

Germany: gold seekers from, 3

Gettysburg campaign: Sam in, 16

Glanton, John: kills man with bowie knife, 1; kills Ranger, 11; Sam joins dubious adventures of, 14; lost treasure of, 15

Goetzmann, Mewes: x

gold: discovered in California, 3, 32n.6; as source of Sam's money, 15

Gold Rush: follows Mexican War, 3

Gorman, Sgt. Tim: Sam duels, **153**, 154

Gothic novel: Sam in tradition of, 28

Goya: 3

Graham, Lawrence P.: 14, 25, 193

Grand Army of the Republic: veterans functions of, ment., 19

Grand Canyon: Sam the first to paint, 14

Grant, U. S.: on Taylor's army, 5; lithograph of, 21, **22**

Gray, Mabry B.: **8**

Gregg, Gen. J. Irving: 16

Grimsley saddle: **73**

Guadalupe Hidalgo, Treaty of. *See* Treaty of Guadalupe Hidalgo

guerrillas, Mexican: army supply lines vulnerable to, 5; Sam observes, **6**, 7, **75**, **76**, **81**; Sam fights, 12, 14, **184**, **192**; attack supply train, 131, 139, 142, **163–164**, **165**; kill U.S. quartermasters, **149**; Sam ordered through country of, **154–162**

Guild, Gov. (Mass.): 34n.61

Gulf of Mexico: W. Scott attacks Vera Cruz from, 7

Gunter, Archibald Clavering: 20

Hacienda Las Chinipas: 187

Hardin, Col. John J.: 133, 137, **138**

Harkinsville: 16

Harmon, Mary: x

Harney: meets Santana, 9

Harney's Dragoons: 12, **47**

Harper's: Butterfield's edition of *My Confession* published by, xi, 1

Harper's Weekly: clippings from, illustrate album, 21

Harrington, Peter: ix

Hays, John Coffee "Jack": **8**; at Monterrey battle, **54**

Hedionda. *See* Rancho Hidiondo [Hedionda]

Henrie, Dan: escapes Mexican lancers, **102**, **103**

Hidalgo Battalion: captured, 133

Higginson family: 15

Higginson, Henry Lee: 15, 33n.50

Hill, Stephen G.: lithograph by, ment., 60

Himalayas, the: Sam in, 15

Hinton, Harwood: ix

Hooker, Gen. Joseph: 21

Horse Fort fight: **192**

horses: of Mexican troops, 5. *See also* Chamberlain, Samuel Emery, horses of

Houston, Sam: at battle of San Jacinto, 1

Huckleberry Finn (novel): 1

Hughes, Lt.: his map of Wool's march, ment., 79

Hughston, Milan: ix

Huseman, Ben W.: ix, x; book by, 137

Illinois: young Sam runs away to, 10–11

Illustrated London News, The: clippings from, illustrate album, 21

Imanuel. *See* Torrescortez/Imanuel (Tuloc architect)

Indians: in Mexican provinces, 3

Iwo Jima: 55

Jackson, David: ix

James, G. P. R.: 28

Johannsen, Robert W.: ix, 35n.77

Johnston, Dr.: on Miñon's dalliance, 14

Jornada del Muerte desert: A. Doniphan crosses, 7
Juvera, Gen. Julian: **116**; at Buena Vista battle, 129, 131, 132, 139

Kailborn, Tom: ix
Kearny, Stephen Watts: volunteer army of, 5; in San Pascual battle, 5–6
Keith, Mary. *See* Chamberlain, Mary Keith
Kelly's Ford, Virginia: Sam wounded at, 16
Kendall, George Wilkins: 35n.77
Kentucky volunteers: surrender of, **101**
King, Capt. Richard: 48
King Ranch: 48
Kiowa Indians: trail through country of, 5
Knepper, Mrs. D. W.: 21
Kohout, Martin: x

Laboyce, Stella: young Sam seduces, 11
Las Chinipas. *See* Hacienda Las Chinipas
Latimer, James A.: 23. *See also* Chamberlain, Tranceita Maria
Lee, Gen. Robert E.: Sam follows, 16
Leutze, Emmanuel: 21; lithograph by, **22**
Life magazine: version of *My Confession* in, xi, 1; Chamberlain watercolors in, 21
Lincoln, Dr. Able: 14
Lipan Indians: 45
Lippard: book by, 28
lithography: 35n.77
Lombardini, Gen. M. M.: **116**, 121, 126
Longfellow, Charles A.: 15
Los Angeles, California: Sam in, 15
Lowell, James Russell: 166

McCarthy, Cormac: ix
McCulloch, Ben: atrocities attributed to, 8; at Buena Vista Ranch, **150**
McDowell (Wool's aide): 95
Malvern Hill: 16
Manifest Destiny: Mexican War highest point of, 3
Marshall, Col. Humphrey: 142
Martin, J. C.: ix
Massachusetts: Sam hospitalized in, 16; Sam appointed assistant quartermaster general of, 19; C. Cushing and politics of, 166
Massachusetts State Penitentiary (Charlestown; Concord): Sam warden of, 19

Matamoros, Mexico: from Fort Brown, **48**
May, Col. Charles: Sam and, 12, 35n.77, **162**; at Hedionda and Saltillo, 113; caricature of, **128**; Rucker's squadron under, 131
Mayer, Brantz: 35n.77
Mears, Capt. Gaston: 188
Mejia, Francisco: **116**
Melville, Herman: 31n.2
mescal: 10
Meschutt, David: ix
Mexican National Archives: xii
Mexicans: Sam's bigotry against, xii
Mexican War: maps, **vi**, **4**; scholars of, ix–x; U.S. empire achieved by, 3; uniforms of Mexican troops in, described, 3, 5; Mitchell's map of, **4**; weapons of, 5; historians of, use *My Confession* as source, 14; last battle of, 21; books dealing with, listed, 37–38
Mexico: Mexican War territorial losses of, 3; symbolically represented, **197**
Mexico City: W. Scott in battles around, 7; J. Hays and assault on, 8; San Cosme Gate of, 21, 22; Sam's paintings of battle for, discussed, 25
Miller, Sgt. Jack: attack led by, **77**
Mine Run Campaign: Sam in, 16
Miñon, Gen.: Saltillo dalliance of, 12, 14; Borland's and Gaines's commands captured by, **101**, 102; Sam spots cavalry of, 109; flares fired by, **113**; retreats with Santa Anna, **169**
Mission Concepción: **42**; Sam made to clean, 11
Mission San Hosea [José]: **42**, **43**
Mission San Ildefonso: burning of, **183**. *See also* San Ildefonso, Palace of
Mississippi Rifles: at Buena Vista battle, 12, 116, 128, 129; Sam rescues Traveina sisters from, 28, **146**; famous V formation of, **122**, **123**, **132**; C. Cushing and, 166
Mississippi River: young Sam steamboats down, 11
Mitchell: map by, **4**
Mixcoac, Mexico: 191
Mojave Desert: 5; Sam crosses, 15
Monclova, Mexico: **69**, **71**; Wool at, 25, **72**; Wool's army marches toward, 66–67, **77**; convent ruins near, **68**
Monks of Monk Hall: 28
Monte Morelos: painting at, 25, **186**; legend of, 185

Monterrey, Mexico: scholars inspect battle site at, ix; map shows, **2**; destruction of, ment., 3; Taylor at, 7, 92; view of, **53**; cathedral at, **60**, **62**, **84**; Sam sketching near, **63**; Wool scouts, **106**; Sam rides through guerrilla country to, 154, **157**, **159**, **160–161**; fandango at, **168**. *See also* Battle of Monterrey; Bishop's Palace

Moore, Merle: ix

Moss, Michael: ix

Motley, Lawrence: 15

Mt. Auburn Cemetery (Old Cambridge, Mass.): Sam buried at, 1, 20

Munroe, Maj. John: at Buena Vista battle, **129**

music: 35n.77

"Mustangers," the: M. Gray commands, 8

Mustang Grey. *See* Gray, Mabry B.

mustangs: mistaken for Santa Anna's army, **88**, **90**

My Confession: draft pages of, ment., ix; project to reprint, xi; Butterfield edits, xi, 1, 26, 31n.1, 34n.69, 123, 185; versions of, ment., xi, 164; first published, 1; described, 10; J. Eisenhower on, 12; historians use as source, 14; chapter openings from, **17**, **69**, **70**; San Jacinto collection in relation to, 21, 26; sold to Old Print Shop, 23; accounts of Monterrey battle in, 25; in romantic tradition, 26; when was it written?, 26; Battle of Buena Vista in, 122, 123; paintings of Tucson, Arizona in, 194

Napoleon: Santa Anna compares himself to, 4, 116; as Hero, 35n.77

National Archives: ix

National Gallery of Art: ix

National Intelligencer (Washington): war accounts in, ment., 7

Necklin (German trooper): 192

Nevada: U.S. gains from Mexican War, 3

Newman, Harry Shaw: 21, 26

Newmarket: 16

New Mexico: U.S. gains from Mexican War, 3

New Orleans *Daily Delta*: war accounts in, ment., 7; on Miñon's dalliance, 14

newspapers: carry guerrilla stories, 7

Nina: Sam paints, **27**, 28, **84**

novels: Sam in tradition of Gothic and romantic, 28

O'Brien, Capt. John Paul: capture of guns of, 12, 28, 125, **126**, **127**, 129; his story, **69**, **74**

O'Callaghan (ferry master): 14

Old Print Shop (New York): San Jacinto Museum buys Chamberlain album from, x, 1, 21, 23

Pacheco, Francisco: **116**; at Buena Vista battle, 121, 132

Palmito Ranch: last Civil War battle at, 16

Parades, Pres. (Mexico): and Mexican War, 5

Parras, Mexico: Wool's army at, 12, **81**, **82–83**; pass near, **79**; possible view of, **93**

Paso del Diablo (Parras): **79**, **80**

Paso de los Pinos: Sam on duty at, **99**

Patterson, Gen.: 189, 195

Pesqueria Grande: **173**, **174**

Pevear, George Irwin: 23. *See also* Chamberlain, Carmeleita Hampton

Plum Creek: J. Hays fights Comanches at, 8

Polk, James K.: N. Trist dismissed by, 7; announces discovery of gold, 32n.6; and C. Cushing, 166

Poolesville, Virginia: Sam captured at, 16

pornography: Sam's use of, 28

Prescott, William Hickling: 25, 28, 35n.77

Presidio, Mexico: 12, **49**; Wool's army at, 48, 67, 71

prostitutes: Sam and, 14, 178

Pugsley, William: x

"Rackensackers." *See* Arkansas Volunteers ("Rackensackers")

Ramos, Mexico: Sam's paintings of, discussed, 28; supply train attacked at, 164

Rancho Agua Nueva: troops march toward, 12, **93**; Wool's army veers to, 86; Wool arrives at Saltillo from, 95; massacre in cave near, **96–97**, **98**; camp at, **107**, **108**, **109**, **144–145**

Rancho Hidiondo [Hedionda]: **104**, **109**, 113; flight from, **114**

Rancho San Jeronimo: skirmish at, **54**

Rancho San Juan Bautista: **152**; guerrillas near, 149

Reams Station: 16

Reid, Samuel C., Jr.: **8**

Rinconada Hills: Sam rides for, **154**, **155**, **156**

Rinconada Pass: troops march to Saltillo via, **94**

Rio Grande: Harney's Dragoons on, 12, **47**; Sam's buffalo soldiers sent to, 16, 19; at Presidio, **49**; U.S. and Mexico symbolically represented across, **197**

Rio Los Palmas [Arroyo de Las]: skirmish at, **77**, **78**

Ritter, Katherine: 11

Ritter's farm (Castroville): Sam at, 11

rogue genre: 28

romance novel: *My Confession* in tradition of, 28

Rosita: Sam paints, **27**, 28, **84**

Rucker, Capt. D. H.: at Buena Vista battle, **130–131**, **140**

Russia: gold seekers from, 3

Sacramento (outside Chihuahua): battle at, ment., 7

saddle. *See* Grimsley saddle

Saddle Mountain (Monterrey): **60**, **63**, 161

St. Louis, Missouri: young Sam in, 11

Salado, Texas: J. Hays fights Comanches at, 8

Salinas, Mexico: fandango at, **64**

Saltillo, Mexico: scholars inspect battle site at, ix; map shows, **2**; Miñon's dalliance at, 12, 14; troops march to, 12, **65**, **86**, **94**; from the north, **86**; cathedral at, **87**; possible view of, **93**; Wool arrives in, **95**; Mexican attack held off at, 113; ruined rancho near, **154**; on Sam's route to Monterrey, **157**; C. Cushing visits, 166

San Angel, Mexico: 191

San Antonio, Texas: Wool marches from, 7, 10, 92; Sam joins Wool's army in, 11; Sam's first painting of, **42**; Military and Main plazas in, **44–45**

San Cosme Church (Mexico City): in lithograph, **22**

San Cosme Gate (Mexico City): U. S. Grant at, 21, **22**

San Diego, California: K. Carson crosses desert from, 5; Sam in, 15

Sandweiss, Martha A.: book by, 137

San Francisco, California: Sam in, 15

San Hosea [José] de Lavacayurea [La Vaqueria]: **91**, **92**

San Ildefonso, Palace of: Sam's painting of, 25, **185**. *See also* Mission San Ildefonso

San Jacinto album: title page to, found, x; described, 10, 20–21, 23, 25–26; Sam works on in his retirement, 19; UT scholars study, 20; in relation to *My Confession*, 21, 26; compared to Brown Military Collection, 23; Sam finishes, 31n.2

San Jacinto Monument: 1

San Jacinto Museum of History: ix; purchases Chamberlain's album, x, 1, 23. *See also* San Jacinto album

San Jacinto. *See* Battle of San Jacinto

San Juan Bautista Ranch. *See* Rancho San Juan Bautista

San Juan Valley (Rinconada): **158**

San Nicholas, Mexico: Carmeleita of, 14, 178, 179

San Pascual. *See* Battle of San Pascual

San Patricio Battalion: deserters from, executed, 25, **190–191**, **196**

Santa Anna, Antonio López de: 12; defeat of, 1, **169**; loses leg, 7; at Monterrey and Buena Vista battles, 7, 132, **134**; as "Napoleon," 35n.77, 116; approach of, 86, 89, 90, 104, 107, 113; and his generals, **116**

Santa Anna's Retreat from Buena Vista (music): 35n.77

Santa Anna's Wooden Leg (music): 35n.77

Santa Caterina rancho: 159, **161**

Santa Fe, New Mexico: conquered, 5; A. Doniphan crosses desert from, 7

Santa Fe trail: Kearny's army down, 5

Santana (Comanche chief): **9**, 12, 25

Sargent, Horace B.: 15, 33n.50; killed, 16

Saturday Review, The: Webb's review of *My Confession* in, 1, 31n.2

Scott, Walter: Sam captivated by heroes of, 10, 28, 31n.2, 184

Scott, Winfield: volunteer army of, 5; attacks Vera Cruz, 7, 195

Scouting Expeditions of McCulloch's Texas Rangers, or, the Summer and Fall Campaigns of the Army of the United States in Mexico—1846, The: 8

Second Illinois Volunteer Regiment: Sam with, 11; at Buena Vista battle, **133**, 137

Second Indiana Regiment: 127, **129**

Second Kentucky Regiment: 137

Selvia, Sandra: x

Seminole War (Florida): American failure in, ment., 5

Seville, Spain: the Alcazar at, 61
Sheridan, Gen.: 16
Sherman, Maj. Thomas W.: orders flogging, 172
Smith, Justin: 14
Smith, Ralph: ix
Smithsonian Institution: gold nugget in, 32n.6
Snooks Ranch (Calif.): 5
Sonora: attempted takeover of, 15
Spain: contrasts with Aztec Mexico, ment., 25; war with France, 74
spurs: guerrilla wears, **6**
steamboats: **48**
Steen, Capt. Enoch S.: 11, **88**, **139**; at Buena Vista battle, 142
Stewart, Rick: book by, 137
Stuart, Jeb: 16
Sturgis, Lt.: reconnaissance led by, **104**, 114
Summerlee Foundation: ix, xi; Chamberlain painting acquired by, 32n.3

Taft, Robert: xi
Taos, New Mexico: conquered, 5
Taylor, Gen. Zachary: volunteers in army of, 5, 7; Monterrey and Buena Vista victories of, 7; Sam with, at Buena Vista, 12, 25; his instructions to Capt. Bragg, 12, 32n.32, **125**; drawing of, discussed, 23, 25; Wool's army marches to meet at Saltillo, 86, 89; orders Butler to Saltillo, 94; sends reconnaissance to Hedionda, 109; at Buena Vista battle, 113, **122**, **124**, 129, 132, **134**; cloud portrait of, **157**; Sam reports with dispatches to, **162**; at play, **163**; sentences V. Galbraith to death, 188; Vera Cruz troops drawn from army of, 195
Texas: independence of, 1; U.S. gains from Mexican War, 3
Texas Mounted Volunteers, First Regiment of: J. Hays commands, 8
Texas Rangers: in Bexar Exchange, 1; J. Hays and, 8; Sam fraternizes with, 11; at Monterrey battle, 12, **54**; at Bishop's Palace, 12, **18**, 25, 32n.25, **56–57**, **58**; Sam regarded as authority on, 20; Sam's paintings of, ment., 25, 26; and derivation of "doughboy," 32n.25; at Buena Vista Ranch, **150**
Texas State Historical Association: ix, xi
Third Indiana Regiment: at Buena Vista battle, 129, 131

Third Massachusetts Militia: Sam joins, 15
Thorpe, Thomas Bangs: 35n.77
Todd, Frederick: 23, 31n.3
Torrescortez/Imanuel (Tuloc architect): 25, 185, 186
Townsend, R. E.: 23, 31n.2
Traveina, Delorious: Sam rescues, 28, **146**, 153
Traveina, Don José: 146
Traveina, Maria Tranceita: Sam rescues, 28, **146**
Treaty of Guadalupe Hidalgo: mentioned, 3, 32n.6; N. Trist and, 7, 10
Trevellion Station raid: 16
Trist, Nicholas P.: and treaty of Guadalupe Hidalgo, 7, 10
Tucson, Arizona: **193**, **194**; Sam leaves with expedition for, 14; Sam's painting of, ment., 25
Tulocs: 25, 185, 186
Twain, Mark: 1; young Sam compared to his Huck, 11
Twiggs, Col.: 195
Tyler, Ron C.: ix

Union, the: first volunteer regiment of, 15
Union army: reorganization of, ment., 16
United States: Mexican War victory of, 3; symbolically represented, **197**
United States Congress: and Treaty of Guadalupe Hidalgo, 7, 10
U.S. Pension Records: on Chamberlain's Civil War wounds, 19–20
U.S. Supreme Court: C. Cushing and, 166
University of Texas: scholars at, study Chamberlain, 20; W. P. Webb of, 1
Uraga, Col. José Lopez: surrender of, **61**
Urrea, José: attacks supply train, 164
Utah: U.S. gains from Mexican War, 3

Veigho, Carmeleita: Chamberlain rescues, 14, **24**, 28, **178**, **179**, **180**, **181**, **182**
Vera Cruz, Mexico: W. Scott attacks, 7, 195
Virginia: Civil War battles in, ment., 16

Walker, Sam: Texans of, at surrender of Monterrey, **60**
Walker, William: trial of, ment., x; recruits Sam, 15

Walnut Springs (near Monterrey): Taylor's camp at, 12, **73**; Sam at, 14, **161**

war correspondents: the first ever, 7

Ward, George: x

Washington, Capt. John M.: at Buena Vista battle, 115, 126

Washington, D.C.: **197**

Washington Crossing the Delaware (painting): 21

Washington Monument: 1

weapons: Sam's collection of, 15, 19

Webb, Walter P.: on *My Confession*, 1, 31n.2

Weber, David: ix

Webster, Marcus "Long": 14

Webster's battery: **160–161**

Westbrook House: 16

West Point: *My Confession* at, ix, 1, 10, 164

West Point Museum: Chamberlain paintings at, ix, 23, 31n.3, 34n.72

Wethersfield, Connecticut: Sam and prison at, x

Whigs: 7

White Cloud (steamboat): 11

Whitehead, Thomas: 11

Whiting, Daniel P.: 35n.77

Whitman, Walt: quoted, 3

Wilson, Lt.: Sam saves, **174**

Winchell, Pvt.: 128

Wool, Gen. John E.: at Buena Vista battle, 7, **118**, **133**; meets with Santana, 9; dispatches to Taylor from, 12; Dr. Johnston with, 14; Sam's painting of, ment., 25; addresses mutineers, **41**; Irish soldier presents arms to, **72**; Hughes's map of his march, ment., 79; arrives at Worth's headquarters, **95**; scouts Monterrey, **106**; orders Sam through guerrilla country, 154

_____ army of: Sam joins, 10, 11; departs San Antonio, **44–45**, 92; crosses Rio Grande, 48; to Monclova, **66–67**, 71, **72**; and Monterrey battle, 67; at Paso del Diablo, **79**, 80; at Parras, **81**, **82–83**; to Saltillo, **86**, **89**

Wool, John E.: Sam in army of, 10

Worcester, Massachusetts: Sam dies in, 20

World War II: 55

Worth, Gen.: troops of, at Monterrey battle, **54**; Wool arrives at headquarters of, 95; at Vera Cruz, 195

Xenophon's Thousand: 7

Yell, Col. Archibald: **142**; Arkansas Volunteers of, **96–97**, 113; reconnaissance force under, 109; at Buena Vista battle, 142

Yuma Indians: J. Glanton and, 14

Zacatecas, Mexico: Sam sketches, **169**, **170**

Zalar, T. J.: ix

Designed and printed at Wind River Press, Austin